Margaret Thatcher: the economics of creative destruction

By Warwick Lightfoot

Copyright © Searching Finance Ltd 2014

The contents of this publication, either in whole or in part, may not be reproduced, stored in a data retrieval system or transmitted in any form or by any means, electronic, mechanical, photocopying, recording or otherwise without the written permission of the copyright owner and publishers. Action will be taken against companies or individual persons who ignore this warning. The information set forth herein has been obtained form sources which we believe to be reliable, but is not guaranteed. The publication is provided with the understanding that the author and publisher shall have no liability for errors, inaccuracies or omissions of this publication and, by this publication, the author and publisher are not engaged in rendering consulting advice or other professional advice to the recipient with regard to any specific matter. In the event that consulting or other expert assistance is required with regard to any specific matter, the services of qualified professionals should be sought.

First published 2014 by Searching Finance Ltd,
ISBN 978-1-907720-76-5

Book design and typesetting by j-views, Kamakura, Japan

About the author

WARWICK LIGHTFOOT IS A PROFESSIONAL ECONOMIST with specialist interests in monetary policy, public expenditure, taxation and labour markets.

Formerly the economics editor of *The European*, he was for many years a frequent contributor to the *Wall Street Journal* and has written for the *Financial Times*, the *Times*, the *Sunday Times*, the *Daily Telegraph*, the *Sunday Telegraph*, and the *Guardian*. His articles on economics and public policy have also been published in specialist journals that range from *Financial World*, *International Economy*, and the *Investors Chronicle* to the *Times Literary Supplement* and the *Journal of Insolvency Practitioners*.

Warwick worked in UK government as Special Adviser to the Chancellor of the Exchequer from 1989 to 1992, initially appointed by Nigel Lawson and later reappointed by John Major and Norman Lamont. He was also Special Adviser to the Secretary of State for Employment, Norman Fowler from 1987 to 1989. He is a Councillor in the Royal Borough of Kensington and Chelsea.

About Searching Finance

SEARCHING FINANCE PUBLISHES books on economics, finance and politics. For more information, please visit www.searchingfinance.com

Contents

Acknowledgements 1

Introduction 3

Chapter 1: Britain in 1979: its Decline and Causes 11

Chapter 2: The Woman Who Was By Turns Patronised and
        Underestimated 15
    Margaret Thatcher as a Parliamentary performer 17
    A tax barrister's skill 18
    Corporate Britain's attitude to Margaret Thatcher 19
    The civil service 20
    The Cabinet colleagues 21

Chapter 3: Breaking with the Post-War Political Consensus in
        Opposition 23

Chapter 4: Changing Britain Profoundly 25

Chapter 5: Inflation, Monetarism and Monetary Conditions 27

Chapter 6: The European Exchange Rate Mechanism 33

Chapter 7: The UK Industrial Relations Problem 41
    The legal framework in 1979 41
    Social alienation and workplace cussedness 42
    The Donovan Report and the failure of In Place of Strife 44
    The Industrial Relations Act, the miners, the three-day week, and Ted
        Heath 45
    Labour's Social Contract, the Grunwick pickets and the Winter of
        Discontent 46
    Trade Union law reform 48
    The miners' strike 50
    Ending the Dock Labour Scheme 55
    The sea change in strikes and days lost through industrial disputes . . 56

Chapter 8: Profits and the Crisis of British Capitalism 59

Chapter 9: Nationalised Industries, the Mixed Economy and Privatisation 63

Chapter 10: A Capital-Owning Democracy 67

Chapter 11: 1976: the End of the Keynesian Consensus 71
    The failure of Keynesian economics 72
    The counter-revolution in political economy 74
    The 1981 Budget and the 364 economists who did not like it 76

Chapter 12: North Sea Oil 79

Chapter 13: The Public Sector Borrowing Requirement Becomes the Public Sector Debt Repayment 85
    The Medium Term Financial Strategy 85
    The tax burden and marginal tax rates 87

Chapter 14: Margaret Thatcher and the City of London: What She Did Not Do 89
    London's international role 92

Chapter 15: The National Health Service, Housing and the Welfare State 97
    Health 97
    Education 99
    Social Security 100
    Housing 101

Chapter 16: Local Government: Centralising to Liberate or Socialistic Planning? 107

Chapter 17: Downfall 115

Chapter 18: Margaret Thatcher's Public Personality and Symbiotic Relationship with her Opponents 119

Chapter 19: A Scientist in Government.................... 123

Chapter 20: The Limits of the Thatcher Agenda 129

Chapter 21: Thatcherism as an Ideology................... 135

Chapter 22: The Economic Legacy of Margaret Thatcher 141

Chapter 23: Alternatives to Thatcher in the Early 1980s 151

Chapter 24: France's *Programme Common*: Neo-Keynesian Economics in One Country.............................. 157

Chapter 25: Margaret Thatcher and Europe................................ 161
   Initially a conventional pragmatic pro-European party leader 161
   A flair for performing on the stage and attracting attention but limited influence... 162
   Awkward personal relationships with European leaders 162
   German reunification in 1990 163
   Fontainebleau Agreement 1984: getting Britain's money back 164

Chapter 26: The French Revolution, the European Social Charter and the Paris Summit 1989....................... 167

Chapter 27: Europe's Role in Margaret Thatcher's Downfall, Sovereignty and the Future of Europe 173
   The debate surrounding the UK's future in the EU 176

Chapter 28: Conclusion 179

Bibliography..................................... 185

Index 189

Margaret Thatcher: the economics of creative destruction

By Warwick Lightfoot

Acknowledgements

THIS BOOK HAS BENEFITED from the extensive literature of political memoirs written by ministers who served in Margaret Thatcher's administrations. The text has benefited from advice from Neill Mitchell, Nicholas Paget-Brown, David Stanton and Clive Tucker. The section on the European Union benefited from the advice of Anthony Teasdale. I am grateful to Professor Jeremy Black, Shelia Chaplin and Dr Richard Wevill for their comments and suggestions about the project. The section looking at science draws heavily on conversations with Lord May FRS and the contributions of Sir Roy Anderson FRS, Professor David Edgerton, Professor Terence Kealey and Sir Crispin Tickell, who participated in the seminar discussing Margaret Thatcher as a scientist in government, held as part of the Science Policy Conference during the Kensington and Chelsea Celebration of Science. I am grateful to Professor Nicholas Crafts of the University of Warwick, and Professor John Van Reenen for their guidance and being able to draw on their research assessing the economic legacy of Margaret Thatcher.

Introduction

THIS BOOK ON MARGARET THATCHER attempts to explain her significance as a politician and to describe how she changed Britain. Margaret Thatcher changed the economic and political argument that had been the bipartisan consensus of the Labour and Conservative parties for a generation. The central arguments were about economics and how the British economy should be run. This book therefore concentrates on the financial crises and the economic challenges that British politicians faced in the 1970s and the economic policies that Margaret Thatcher and her colleagues developed to respond to them. It is written from the perspective of an economist, who worked as a political adviser at the Department of Employment and at the Treasury during her third administration. Margaret Thatcher and what came to be considered the British experiment in economic policy can only be properly understood in the context of what had gone wrong in British economic policy in the 1950s and 1960s. It was a response to the collapse of the Keynesian model and to the failure of an agenda of social democratic reform that was attempted in various guises, by Labour governments, and to a considerable extent by Conservative governments as well, in the 1960s and 1970s.

Margaret Thatcher's death after a difficult and sad decline elicited many generous tributes even from her political opponents, who had understandable reasons to be less than kind, given the bitterness surrounding much of the government business that she transacted. There was one interesting gloss or revision to history, however, which deserves to be corrected. It goes something like this: Margaret Thatcher transformed Britain by doing necessary things; and of course these things would inevitably have had to be done, but they could have been done with greater emollience and much less social and political bitterness. This is a reading of history through rose-tinted cataracts. What makes Margaret Thatcher remarkable is that she did make economic changes that were necessary and overdue. Other governments had tried and failed to do so, because they faced entrenched, bitter and potentially violent opposition. They incurred anger, yet failed to secure the changes that were needed. The changes could not be made without confronting bitter opposition. Margaret Thatcher's predecessors, such as Harold Wilson and Edward Heath were not immune from controversy. Edward Heath, in particular was an object of intense loathing and contempt when he was Prime Minister. Much of the opprobrium that Margaret Thatcher acquired arose from the fact that she succeeded where her immediate predecessors had patently failed.

This book is neither a history of her government nor the story of her life. It does not attempt to explore the high politics of the Conservative Party, or to chronicle the dramatic episodes that punctuated her period in office. As with President De Gaulle's tenure in France, Margaret Thatcher's governments experienced a series of crises of regime. Among them were the rows with the 'wets' in the Cabinet over economic policy in 1981, the Falklands War in 1982, and Westland and the Heseltine resignation in 1986. This monograph attempts to identify the key changes that Margaret Thatcher made and to locate them in their broader political, social and economic contexts.

In the process it seeks to illustrate why Margaret Thatcher was such an unusual figure among British politicians. It is written by someone who admired Margaret Thatcher as a person and came to have an abiding respect for her as Prime Minister. This respect reflected the vim, seriousness and sheer application that she put into the job. Margaret Thatcher brought what can only be called a destructive excitement to politics. Arguments and institutions that plainly needed to be challenged and dismembered are likely in normal circumstances to be left alone, on the 'let sleeping dogs lie' principle. Under Margaret Thatcher they were challenged and taken apart. Whether it was the metropolitan county authorities or the rules preventing solicitors from arguing cases in the higher courts, thereby protecting the bar from competition, Margaret Thatcher had a tendency to make things happen. She also had a powerful style of argument that was at once forensic and lucid, in a funny way, made all the more direct by her unusual relationship with the English language, in terms of conventional grammar and syntax. This book will try to capture the vivid character of Margaret Thatcher's political personality, because it is necessary to appreciate it, in order to understand much of the controversy surrounding her and because it is part of the explanation of her extraordinary capacity to transform the terms of debates that had been previously settled for many years.

What will not be considered here in anything other than a passing mention is Margaret Thatcher's role in international affairs at the height of the Cold War. The Falklands war will always be remembered. A potential foreign policy humiliation that could have destroyed her in the way that Suez destroyed Sir Anthony Eden, it was turned into a personal and political triumph. Politically the Falklands War was hugely important, because it gave the Conservative Party support for reasons that had nothing to do with its economic agenda. That support politically rescued Margaret Thatcher. It gave her a renewed mandate for economic reform and it gave time for the reforms to yield obvious benefits. In the early 1980s Margaret Thatcher's most perceptive, often Marxian, critics recognised that her policies were coherent and necessary, in order to make a market economy function properly, but they take time to show visible results, and in the meantime, the electoral cycle would probably abort the Conservative economic experiment. The Falklands War changed that. By 1982 the economy was already recovering and inflation was falling, but the electoral position of the Conservative Party looked grim. There were people who identified a change in the political weather before the Falklands War, but to most people this evidence was obscure. Margaret Thatcher's determination and victory in the Falklands War greatly enhanced her international and domestic political standing. The victory reversed the malaise of the Suez debacle and gave the British political establishment renewed confidence.

Margaret Thatcher was unique among post-war British prime ministers in having good working relationships with both the leaders of the USA and the USSR, President Ronald Reagan and General Secretary Mikhail Gorbachev. It was the personal friendship that she struck up with Mikhail Gorbachev that enabled her significantly to contribute to the ending of the Cold War. In many respects she was fortunate. She was there as the socialist planned economies were evidently failing to deliver acceptable living standards and continued to exhibit egregious inhumane totalitarian control over their people. The 'look at the Soviet Union and the Eastern European economies and see how attractive socialism is' line of argument was a political gift for any Conservative politician. Margaret Thatcher made full use of the Soviet bogey. She used it to good effect in domestic politics. She was fortunate to be a significant world leader when the Cold War ended and Soviet control of central and Eastern Europe was dismantled in 1989. Insofar as the Prime Minister was able to cut an effective figure on the world stage, this was significantly due to the international perception that she was taking necessary and difficult economic measures and the economy was appearing to respond. Yet there is no doubt that her remorseless ideological critique of Communism, her hawkish views on defence spending and the extraordinary figure that she cut as the world's first woman leader of a major advanced country were important.

Margaret Thatcher: The economics of creative destruction

Over 11 years is a long time to be in power, and Margaret Thatcher was always in power, not just in office. She brought about fundamental changes in the ownership structure of industry through denationalisation, in industrial relations through trade union law reform, radically changed and lowered the structure of marginal income tax rates and presided over an audacious programme of monetary disinflation. The Medium Term Financial Strategy (MTFS) represented a profound change in the approach to economic management. These policies involved very painful transition costs. There is no doubt that Margaret Thatcher had a bold agenda in 1979. It is also probably accurate to say, she not only accomplished it, but went beyond that agenda by the time she left Downing Street in November 1990. Before she was elected she knew what she wanted to do and moved the country further in her chosen direction than most people expected.

The big question is: was it worth it and did the changes yield the benefits that were expected of them? In some of the political debate the genuine improvement in the UK economy that resulted from these policies was exaggerated. Margaret Thatcher and her ministers did not create an economic miracle. That is not in any way to underestimate or undersell what was achieved. Her policies changed the UK economy from a position of relative economic decline that periodically threatened to fall into absolute decline in the decades that followed the end of the Second World War in 1945, to one where the economy performed in the manner expected of a mature advanced OECD economy. If anything, it appeared to perform slightly better. This is a massive achievement, and the policies that made it possible are still offering economic dividends almost a quarter of a century after Margaret Thatcher left power. Micro-economic measures taken to improve the supply performance of the economy take a long time before they begin to yield benefits. They continue to yield benefits many years after they were enacted.

The micro-economic measures taken by Margaret Thatcher's governments contributed to a significant improvement in the structure and flexibility of the economy. This has been evident since the start of the great recession following the credit crunch in 2007. The UK economy suffered a huge adverse shock, losing over 7 per cent of output. Yet the labour market has performed very well. It has exhibited a high degree of wage flexibility where real wages have adjusted to the adverse shock, with the result that private sector employment has held up well. There has been a price adjustment rather than a quantity adjustment. This is what ministers and members to the Government Economic Service thought ought to happen. They were only too aware of how inflexible the UK labour market was in the early 1980s. Instead of real wage growth adjusting in the face of an adverse economic shock wages continued to increase, while employment fell and unemployment rose, even as output began to recover.

Margaret Thatcher was a unique figure in British politics. She possessed an electrifying quality that attracted and repelled in equal measure. Clever, possessed of expertise unusual in politics at the highest level, she was always a striking figure, who in public possessed a form of poise that in itself amounted to political authority. The word 'imperious' does not do justice to the command and authority exuded from her personal manner. It was hard not to be fascinated by her and over more than 35 years she has become a prism through which people refract their views and commentary on contemporary society. This process of often hostile refraction goes far beyond conventional politics into the arts, culture and even sport.

Margaret Thatcher had a sort of corrosive efflorescence that does not so much cast a shadow a quarter of a century since she left office, or to be more accurate, was ejected from power, but rather intrudes into much contemporary discussion and continues to shape modern sensibility. This is not the effect of her own actions, views and her direct legacy, as people continuing to respond to her record and legacy, as they perceive it, in an atavistic manner. Appreciating her extraordinary personality is necessary, in order, to understand what she did, why she did it and what her legacy is. It is also the key to understanding, to borrow from the language of neo-classical economics, what could be called her 'super-normal' legacy.

The greatest tribute paid to Margaret Thatcher was made shortly before she died in April 2013. Denis Healey in the Easter double edition of the *New Statesman* gave an interview and repeated what he had said about her in his memoirs. A Labour MP, Charlie Pannel, had got to know Margaret Thatcher as a new MP in the 1960s and he told Healey to watch out for her, saying, as Healey recalled, " 'She is good looking and politically brilliant' and she was". She was the first woman British Prime Minister, but more than that, she was a most capable Prime Minister.

Chapter 1: Britain in 1979: its Decline and Causes

THE STARTING POINT for understanding why Margaret Thatcher is important and how her government represents a transforming event in British politics is to appreciate Britain's post-war economic and political decline. This decline is best illustrated by the valedictory dispatch sent from the retiring British ambassador to France, Sir Nicholas Henderson to the Labour Foreign Secretary, Dr David Owen, on 31 March 1979, entitled *Britain's Decline: Its Causes and Consequences*. Henderson's dispatch marshals compelling evidence of the UK's relative economic decline compared to France and the Federal Republic of Germany – the old West Germany. Henderson showed that in 1954 French GDP was 22 per cent and German GDP was 9 per cent lower the UK's; and how by 1977 French GDP was 34 per cent higher and German GDP was 61 per cent higher. He wrote that:

'In the mid-1950s we were still the strongest European power militarily and economically. It is our decline since then in relation to our European partners that has been so marked. We are scarcely in the same economic league as the Germans and French. We talk of ourselves without shame as being one of the less prosperous countries in Europe. The prognosis for the foreseeable future is discouraging. If present trends continue we shall be overtaken in GDP per head by Italy and Spain well before the end of the century.'

Henderson attributed this economic decline to weak productivity growth and a lower level of productivity in the UK. He identifies several contributory causes for this poor productivity. British management lacked the professionalism of that in other advanced economies. This was partly the traditional prestige of working in the City of London and in the public service in the UK, but it was also a function of weak financial incentives. Henderson cites the example of the pay of a middle-grade manager when adjusted for taxes and differences in taxes and living costs being nearly twice as high in France and Germany as in the UK. The head of Peugeot-Citroën enjoyed a salary "over twice that of the Chairman of British Leyland, leaving many fringe benefits out of the account. The maximum tax on his salary is 60 per cent whereas that on Mr Edwardes's 83 per cent".

The second major cause identified by Henderson was the trade unions and the structure of labour relations. Unlike contemporary Europe, the UK had a tradition of craft unions with a strong temptation to pursue sectional interests at the expense of another union or of the company as a whole. This was aggravated by the number of separate unions in the UK. There were 17 major integrated unions in Germany and six major union confederations in France, compared to 115 unions affiliated to the TUC. This made the negotiation of workable pay and other arrangements more difficult. In addition collective agreements in Germany and France were legally binding and enforceable in law. In the UK 50 per cent of the labour force was in trade unions compared to 22 per cent in France and 44 per cent in Germany. The efficiency of individual plants in the UK was further undermined by the powerful role of local shop stewards.

'There is no shop floor control over production in France as there is in Britain. No French manager thinks twice about changing people's duties or their timetables if that is required for efficiency, nor does he hesitate to *install new machinery and instruct people that from Monday onwards they will be working at x instead of y. Neither in France nor Germany has responsibility for production shifted out of the hands of management into those of trade union representatives.'*

Henderson shows that strikes were a much bigger problem in the UK than in France and Germany and the problem had got worse. The number of days lost through industrial stoppages in 1957 was 69,000 in Germany, in France 3,506,000, and 6,012,000 in the UK. In 1977 the UK lost 10,142,000 days in strikes compared to 2,434,000 in France and 86,000 in Germany. As well as the higher number of strikes in Britain, they appeared to be more effective in achieving their immediate trade union objective. Henderson quotes his embassy's labour attaché saying that 'the Labour Counsellor here cannot think of a single strike in France in the past two years that has achieved its objective.' Henderson, however, goes on to make the point that while unions in the UK were influential, made ready use of the strike weapon and often got their way in disputes, the overall results for workers were disappointing. In the UK, compared to France and Germany, 'not only are real wages lower but hours of work are longer.'

Much of this extraordinary dispatch is then occupied with the usual matters that concern ambassadors, principally the handling of Britain's relationship with Europe. Among them are the intensification of the Bonn-Paris relationship, partly reflecting perceived British economic weakness, the US commitment to promoting European integration, the expediency of loosening the Commonwealth commitment, a constructive attitude to the idea of Europe, and the post-war misjudgements of continuing to play a world role and the failure 'to cut our coat according to our cloth', as well as failing to take a lead in constructing the framework for European integration as the Messina conference in 1955. Its opening sentence is very much the statement of an ambassador concerned about having the economic and financial base to give effect to his diplomacy. 'Since Mr Ernest Bevin made his plea a generation ago for more coal to give weight to his foreign policy our economic decline has been such as to sap the foundations of our diplomacy.' Henderson also recognised that identifiably lower GDP per capita was resulting in noticeably lower standards of living and poorer public services in the UK compared to France and Germany.

Nicholas Henderson was frustrated and angry about Britain's relative economic and political decline. While many British people shared that bitterness, there were many people in important positions of public responsibility who were content laconically to accept and preside over it. Indeed they were often skilled at constructing elegant explanations that suggested that it either was not real or that it was desirable, even civilised. Henderson directly refers to what he calls these 'pastoral apologists' who 'argue that the British way of life, with ingenuity and application devoted to leisure rather than work, is superior to that elsewhere and is in any case what people want'. Twelve years later Noel Annan, a quintessential member of the British establishment, published a book, *Our Age*, that surveyed his generation. Lord Annan painted a rich and an unattractive portrait of élite personalities who were self-regarding and lacked the moral and intellectual courage to confront Britain's post-war economic and political challenges.

The British civil service openly explained in the 1970s that the task of the government was to manage decline. What is interesting about Sir Nicholas Henderson is that he did not share that view. Although he was very pessimistic about the UK's prospects in 1979, he recognised that if Germany and France could 'have managed to achieve such progress in so relatively a short a time' it should be possible for Britain to do so 'if there is the necessary leadership.' Margaret Thatcher explicitly rejected any notion of managed decline. Her purpose was to reverse it. The Henderson Valedictory Dispatch remains the best summary of the position that she confronted in 1979.

Chapter 2: The Woman Who Was By Turns Patronised and Underestimated

ONE OF THE PECULIARITIES OF MARGARET THATCHER'S CAREER was that, although she was an outstandingly capable person, she was repeatedly underestimated. This was clearly the case during the Conservative leadership election in 1975. The rules agreed for the election made it very difficult for Ted Heath to be defeated. As Alec Douglas-Home, the former Conservative Prime Minister who devised them put it, short of filling in the ballot papers for Heath, Ted was as safe as could be expected. When the only significant candidate to emerge was Margaret Thatcher, the general assumption was that 'Ted is safe'. It is hard now to convey the shock when the news broke that she had outpolled the former Conservative Prime Minister Ted Heath on the first ballot, and that Ted Heath was withdrawing from the contest.

Next it was the turn of the Parliamentary Labour Party. The night she was elected Leader of the Conservative Party the Labour Party underestimated her. There are many stories of Labour ministers buying drinks and congratulating themselves on the Tories' mistake in electing her as Leader. Neil Kinnock bought Norman Lamont a drink and commiserated that the Tories would be out of power for 20 years. It was not just that she was a woman, but *that* woman. The former Secretary of State for Education, Milk Snatcher Thatcher, once described by the *Sunday Times* colour supplement as 'Britain's most hated Cabinet Minister'. She was the kind of Tory leader who would achieve resoundingly increased majorities in suburban Surbiton and Bournemouth, but would fail to appeal to key marginal constituencies in the West Midlands and Northwest. There was the grating voice, the clothes, the hats and the whole 1970s 'gin and jags chic of Chelsea meets the Home Counties'. It was as if Margot from the TV programme *The Good Life* was seriously attempting to become Prime Minister.

Prime Minister's Question Time is difficult for any Leader of the Opposition and it was difficult for Margaret Thatcher. She initially faced the Labour Prime Minister Harold Wilson, the consummate parliamentary performer of his generation. At one of her earlier outings Margaret Thatcher asked a prolix question about public spending. The previous day the press had extensively covered 'a Sunday for Monday piece' of photographs of the Leader of the Opposition painting and decorating her weekend flat in a country house in Kent. After she had finished the tedious question, Wilson began replying by offering her retrospective congratulations on her birthday and said, 'as for the paint problem, the answer is to try turps'. It brought the house down. Shortly before he resigned, Wilson delivered an effective and excoriating speech mocking Margaret Thatcher's first steps towards policy-making that seriously broke with the post-war consensus advocating a monetary approach to inflation. Wilson compared her to Heath, ridiculing the Conservative Party for abandoning 'Selsdon Man' only to embrace 'Piltdown Woman'. Wilson was funny and patronising and he spoke for much of the British establishment.

James Callaghan, the Labour Prime Minister who followed Wilson in 1976, perfected an effective parliamentary manner that exuded an avuncular authority and patronisingly dismissed the Leader of the Opposition. In one encounter Callaghan used the famous lines from Dryden on the Duke of Buckingham, 'that in the course of one revolving moon he was chemist, fiddler, statesman and buffoon'. The Parliamentary Labour Party's tone is as well illustrated by the reaction of Labour MPs to Margaret Thatcher's appointment of the wealthy Mrs Sally Oppenheim as Shadow Secretary for Prices and Consumer Affairs. Labour MPs laughed, commenting that the only shop floor she had been on was Harrods. Of course, it was not only Labour MPs that underestimated her, plenty of her own party did. Many of her Shadow Cabinet did and several backbench MPs. Some Conservative MPs who were strong supporters of Ted Heath went around saying to anyone who would listen that she was 'mad'.

Margaret Thatcher as a Parliamentary performer

IT WAS THEREFORE PARADOXICAL that Margaret Thatcher's direct path to power turned out to be through a classic parliamentary victory, secured on the floor of the House of Commons. No government had been forced from office on a confidence motion for more than 50 years. The failure of the yes vote on devolution in Scotland to secure the necessary support of two-fifths of the electorate resulted in the Labour Government laying orders for the repeal of its own devolution measure. The SNP tabled a no confidence motion that the official Opposition took over. In the debate Margaret Thatcher displayed a withering contempt for the Labour Government's record and demonstrated her authority as a parliamentary performer in debate. She displayed the qualities that would become so familiar when they were invested with the full authority of a Prime Minister commanding a majority in the House of Commons and an electoral mandate.

The Woman Who Was By Turns Patronised and Underestimated

A tax barrister's skill

MARGARET THATCHER'S COMMAND of the House of Commons, taste for forensic detail and repartee in debate should never have been underestimated. She benefited from her training and experience as a barrister practicing at the tax bar. Even before she became Leader of the Opposition, as a junior Shadow Treasury Spokesman, debating the 1975 Finance Bill clause by clause she had demonstrated astonishing parliamentary flair. This was the bill that introduced Capital Transfer Tax in place of conventional estate duty. The exchanges in Hansard between Margaret Thatcher and the Labour Chancellor of the Exchequer provide a flavour of the bitterness of that debate.

Denis Healey: We on the Government side listened as intently as did her Right Hon. and Hon. friends to her speech to discover what slogan might be emblazoned on her campaign banner, because we know that she seeks – this is an honourable ambition – the right to lead her party and the country towards the 21st century. The fact is that she went backwards and not forwards, to one of the oldest slogans in political history.

The fact is that she emerged in this debate as La Pasionaria of privilege. She showed that she has decided, as the Daily Express *said this morning, to see her party tagged as the party of the rich few. I believe that she and her party will regret it.*

Margaret Thatcher: I wish I could say that (Denis Healey) the Chancellor of the Exchequer had done himself less than justice. Unfortunately, I can only say that I believe he has done himself justice. Some Chancellors are macro-economic. Other Chancellors are fiscal. This one is just plain cheap. When he rose to speak yesterday we on this side were all amazed how one could possibly get to be Chancellor of the Exchequer and speak for his Government, knowing so little about existing taxes and so little about the proposals which were coming before Parliament. If this Chancellor can be Chancellor, anyone in the House of Commons could be Chancellor.

I had hoped that the Right Hon. gentleman had learned a lot from this debate. Clearly he has learnt nothing. Whatever the theory of this tax, which will have a very far-reaching effect upon the country, he might at least address himself to the practical effects, because it will affect not only the one in a thousand to whom he referred but everyone, including people born like I was with no privilege at all. It will affect us as well as the Socialist millionaires.

Whatever the theory, this tax is fundamentally damaging in two ways. First it damages the economic structure of our society by its effect on private businesses, on farming, on woodlands and on shipping. Secondly, it damages the very nature of our society by concentrating power and property in the hands of the State and of those politicians whose only ambition is the pursuit of power for its own sake. We believe that the future of freedom is inseparable from a wide distribution of private property among the people, not concentrating it into the hands of politicians.'

Any astute politician or political commentator who had followed the exchanges between Margaret Thatcher and Labour Treasury ministers during the debate of the 1975 Finance Act would have been in no doubt of her command of detail, her capacity to use her training as a barrister to deploy technical details in a forensic manner and her flair as a parliamentary performer, who could set arguments of technical detail in a wider political and ideological context.

Corporate Britain's attitude to Margaret Thatcher

BEFORE SHE TOOK OFFICE as Prime Minister, during the Winter of Discontent in 1979, when the writing for the Labour Government was on the wall, there was widespread discussion about how Margaret Thatcher was not up to the job. At City lunch tables and in directors' dining room suites, the great and the good of 1970s corporate Britain in let it be known that Margaret Thatcher did not have what it would take. Margaret Thatcher was too extreme, she could not work with the unions, and her Cabinet would have to control her. There was so much of this talk about, that Alan Watkins, the political columnist writing in the *Observer* and firmly on the left, wrote a column explaining that she would not be that bad, because all politicians are pretty much the same.

The civil service

THE OFFICIAL MACHINE WAS READY in Whitehall. They had dealt with a previous Conservative Prime Minister, Ted Heath, who had entered office with a radical agenda and they were ready to help Thatcher to see sense. They were prepared to explain the benefits of income policies, the importance of working with the trade unions and much else. The first four years of her administration were one bruising encounter after another for the administrative civil service. The civil service was used to guiding ministers away from the worst excesses of their party's agenda. Had they not successfully confined Tony Benn and his Alternative Economic Strategy acolytes in a ministerial cul-de-sac for five years? As one young Treasury official put it, ministers would just have to learn to accommodate themselves to the advice of their officials, as though the democratic mandate of the Government were an inconvenient irrelevance.

There were all sorts of stories throughout Whitehall of rows and incidents between the Prime Minister and silky permanent secretaries, who reassuringly tried to convince her that things could either not be done or should not be pursued. Perhaps the most bruising were the meetings where senior officials were under-briefed and thought they could get away with not knowing the facts about the policies their departments were notionally running. A permanent secretary at the Department of Energy was famously incapable of explaining the generating capacity of Battersea power station to the satisfaction of the Prime Minister. At the Department of Employment one senior official was incapable of answering her question about the way benefits were up-rated. As he explained to colleagues afterwards, he had simply never thought about it. Some of the cleverest, best educated and, by their lights, most successful men of their generation were contradicted and challenged on facts, figures and principle by a woman who in any other circumstances they would have patronised or dismissed. What was worse, she was straightforwardly intelligent, was normally as well if not better briefed on the matter at hand than they were, and often had sought additional, albeit sometimes quirky, further advice outside the official machine. These encounters were never costless for the traditional civil service. It was well known that the Prime Minister had a blacklist of officials whose promotion she remembered to block. Nothing quite brings a government bureaucracy to heel as the determined and sometimes unfair application of malicious political power, where appointments are involved. Margaret Thatcher came to appreciate greatly the efficiency and help of the permanent civil service, but it was definitely achieved by the effective and cruel, yet necessary, wielding of the handbag in a manner that probably had not been expected in 1979.

The Cabinet colleagues

THE FOURTH GROUP TO UNDERESTIMATE HER was that of her colleagues in the Shadow Cabinet and in the Government. Margaret Thatcher had become Leader of the Conservative Party as the standard bearer of a peasants' revolt. Hardly any of her Shadow Cabinet had voted for her. When she formed her first administration in 1979 it was not so different from a coalition government. The 'dries' who supported her economic policies were in economically important departments – Treasury, Trade and Industry and Energy – while the 'wets' were confined in the Foreign Office, the Ministry of Agriculture and doing jobs such as leading the House of Commons and taking care of the Duchy of Lancaster and the arts. In government the Cabinet was slowly reconstructed in a manner closer to her liking. But the truth is, although she succeeded in achieving a co-operative Cabinet, it was never a wholly reliable body. Often she was forced through practical circumstance to promote able people who by no stretch of the imagination could be considered as obvious prosecutors of her ideas and prejudices. The true extent of this was revealed during the year before the Prime Minister's resignation when she was forced to go along with membership of the ERM. And of course it was on obvious display during the awkward and fraught exchanges that took place between the Prime Minister and her Cabinet the evening before her resignation. The reason why there was normally no woman in the Cabinet is that several of the obvious appointees had gone out of their way to make it clear that they were her internal political enemies.

Chapter 3: Breaking with the Post-War Political Consensus in Opposition

BEFORE SHE WON POWER in the 1979 election, Margaret Thatcher as Leader of the Opposition had already broken the mould of post-war politics. She had demanded a monetary approach to inflation, the ending of prices and incomes policy, and she had openly talked about the need as she saw it to recognise business and to reward success. This was most vividly expressed in a speech in New York in 1975 when she said that some of our children can grow taller than others. In the mid-1970s this was immensely provocative. It was an explicit rejection of egalitarianism. She made it clear that a future Conservative Government would reverse significant pieces of Labour legislation, such as the Community Land Act and the Capital Transfer Tax on gifts *inter vivo*. More than that, Margaret Thatcher set out a different philosophy and vision for Britain. This was based on reducing the size of the state, lowering tax rates and creating the conditions for widespread home ownership and the possession of savings, investments and pensions. She caricatured the alternative as a 'pocket money society' where the state makes all the big decisions in a person's life – schools, housing, health and pension, only leaving small things such as the choice of the colour of the curtains to the individual.

This was not Mr Wilson and Mr Heath or a choice between Tweedledum and Tweedledee. This was a frontal assault on post-war collectivism and an assertion of the merits of personal freedom, the benefits of free markets and private enterprise. In 1976 Margaret Thatcher was fully engaged in a political debate that was, as Oliver Cromwell might have said, about the 'fundamentals' not the 'circumstantials' of politics. The opportunity to enter into such a debate reflected the atmosphere of malaise and crisis in the 1970s. Inflation of 25 per cent, rising unemployment and a Public Sector Borrowing Requirement of 10 per cent of GDP created a sense of sustained economic crisis. The opportunity to shift the ideological argument also resulted from the agenda being pursued by the trade unions and the hard left within the Labour Party.

The trade unions had insisted on the repeal of the Industrial Relations Act of 1971 and the passage of Trade Union and Labour Relations Act in 1976 that further extended the immunities that the unions enjoyed from the law. As well as extending the closed shop, the Marxian radicalisation of the trade unions and their perfection of blacking, secondary picketing and flying picketing combined with the willingness of many workers and other people involved, to use violence and violent intimidation, meant that when Margaret Thatcher quoted Dicey on the importance of the rule of law she was not making a recondite comment, but a provocative statement. Moreover, while Margaret Thatcher, Sir Keith Joseph, Sir Geoffrey Howe, Nigel Lawson and Nicholas Ridley were developing a radical right-wing economic agenda based on markets and disinflation, the Left was developing the Alternative Economic Strategy. The command economies of Eastern Europe were its inspiration. This Bennite agenda later found its fullest expression in the 1983 Labour election manifesto. Margaret Thatcher ended up liking Tony Benn in his retirement, and called him a good old-fashioned patriot, but that was not how he seemed in the 1970s.

Margaret Thatcher: The economics of creative destruction

Chapter 4: Changing Britain Profoundly

MARGARET THATCHER'S GOVERNMENTS changed Britain profoundly. The biggest changes related to the economy, where they were intended to halt relative economic decline. Her policies went a long way towards doing so. The UK returned to performing in the way that a mature advanced economy might be expected to do so, in marked contrast to the 20 years before Margaret Thatcher took her Party to power. What her governments did to bring this about is the substance of this book. As well as changing the structure of the economy, her governments made big changes to a range of public institutions and professional organisations and showed that intractable problems could be addressed through change, and what appeared to be fixtures with no good purpose could be removed. Good examples of both are the abolition of the Metropolitan county councils, the Greater London Council (GLC) and the Inner London Education Authority (ILEA), and the reforms to the legal system that gave solicitors the right to appear in the higher courts, breaking the bar's monopoly on advocacy.

As part of the reform of traditional institutions such as the London Stock Exchange, known as the Big Bang, Margaret Thatcher brought about a change in attitudes and a change in sensibility that was much more influential than the actual policy changes themselves, or indeed the attitudes and mentalities that she was actually seeking to promote. This change in sensibility was principally a meritocratic disposition, a celebration of enterprise, the embracing of business, change and success. The promotion and celebration of an enterprise culture by Margaret Thatcher is at the heart of the atavistic response to her legacy. This continues to shape and define modern cultural expression, if only as a sort of comfort blanket of revulsion that is delivered before anything is done or said.

In the post-war period after 1945 the performance of the UK economy had been distinguished by several features. There was a stop-go cycle where very high levels of employment were sustained with increasing problems of inflation, pressures on the balance of payments and a periodically devaluing exchange rate. Relative economic performance was marked by slow rates of growth that were consistent with weak productivity and low rates of return on capital and investment. By 1975 the stop-go cycle of the 1950s and 1960s seemed positively benign as stagflation took hold and prices rose by over 25 per cent in one year, while unemployment rose. The following sections will look at monetary policy and inflation, the labour market and trade union reform, the public finances, supply-side reform incentives and the ending of the mixed economy through Margaret Thatcher's programme of denationalisation. The policies developed to deal with these areas combined to yield a profound change that warrants the description 'transformative'.

Chapter 5: Inflation, Monetarism and Monetary Conditions

IN 1979 BRITAIN HAD HAD AN INFLATION PROBLEM for about 20 years. In the 1970s it shared it with most of the advanced economies in the OECD, but it was worse in the UK than in any major economy, with the possible exception of Italy. In the late 1950s Harold Macmillan's Conservative Government became concerned about creeping inflation and set up a committee under Lord Radcliffe to investigate it, that reported in 1959. The best illustration of the effects of slow and rising peacetime inflation could be found in the financial markets. Gilts had been bought by 'trustee type institutions' – Oxbridge colleges, the Church of England, charities and pension funds. As inflation rose, the real value of the fixed incomes from bonds fell and there was a portfolio adjustment. Investors moved out of gilts and into equities. This created the 'reverse yield gap,' first identified by George Ross Goobey, the general managing director of the Imperial Tobacco pension fund, in 1956. Before then, the dividends on equities was normally higher than yield on very safe government bonds, such as gilts. This was the start of a 50-year epoch in investment management – the so-called 'cult of equity'.

Before Lord Radcliffe's committee reported, Prime Minister Macmillan had resolved to do nothing much about inflation, because he was concerned with maintaining full employment. In Macmillan's judgement, and that of most of his officials, this required adherence to the Keynesian formula for ensuring that there was enough demand in the economy to secure full employment, with the Government making up any deficiency in demand by changes in government spending and deficits. This approach had been set out by the wartime Conservative Chancellor, Sir Kingsley Wood in the 1941 Budget. In 1958 the Chancellor of the Exchequer Peter Thorneycroft wanted to cut public spending to curb inflation, but the Prime Minister did not back him. The result was that the Chancellor and his whole team of Treasury ministers resigned. The clear message from this episode was that Chancellors who sought to address inflation by controlling government spending and borrowing and were prepared to use higher interest rates would not get the political backing of the Prime Minister to do so.

This changed with Margaret Thatcher. One of her first appointments, on winning the Conservative Party leadership in 1975, was to make Lord Thorneycroft Chairman of the Conservative Party. Peter Thorneycroft's appointment was the embodiment of her rejection of inflation and the Butskellite consensus. It was an explicit rejection of Harold Macmillan's legacy and the post-war Conservative approach to economic management.

By the time Margaret Thatcher had become Leader of the Opposition there was already an intense international debate about inflation and its causes. This was led by Milton Friedman. In the UK the argument was presented by two economists writing in the *Times*, Tim Congdon and Peter Jay, and by Samuel Britton, the economic commentator of the *Financial Times*. In the City of London, where much of the first proper monetary analysis was being undertaken in the UK, it was led by Gordon Pepper, the research partner at the stockbroker Greenwell Montagu, and presented in the firm's famous *Monetary Bulletin*. Much of this work in the UK was a direct response to the monetary explosion measured by M3 between 1971 and 1973. This followed from the deregulation of the banks as a result of changes brought in as part of Competition Credit and Control in 1971. In practice this made it easier for banks to lend and resulted in a lot of credit and little control. It was aggravated by Ted Heath's neo-Keynesian dash for growth. Even Ted Heath's Shadow Chancellor, Robert Carr – Margaret Thatcher's boss on the Conservative Shadow Treasury team – said in late 1974 that he wanted better control of the money supply.

Getting inflation down was Margaret Thatcher's priority. The *Right Approach to the Economy* published in 1977 was clear: 'Our prime and overriding objective is to unwind the inflationary coils which have gripped our economy'. This was to be brought about by 'the gradual reduction in the rate of growth of the money supply, in line with firm monetary targets', supported by a revaluation of the exchange rate supported the effect of North Sea oil on the balance of payments and a reduction of domestic and international government borrowing. This was an agenda for sustained disinflation brought about by tight monetary conditions. Monetary policy was given the key role, and monetary targets were to be used to reduce inflationary expectations. In the *Right Approach to the Economy* in 1977 Margaret Thatcher and the Conservative Party embraced 'monetarism'.

In government the Conservatives carried out what she said they would when they had been in Opposition. A very tight monetary squeeze was imposed on the UK economy that brought about sharp and unexpected disinflation. It was very successful. Three things combined to reduce inflation: high nominal interest rates, high and rising real interest rates and an exchange rate that was rising sharply. The exchange rate was driven by several factors: the impact of North Sea oil on the external balance, the high and rising real interest rates, and the international financial markets' enthusiasm for a Prime Minister and Conservative Government that spoke their language sometimes better, than they did.

Any significant process of reducing inflation incurs transition costs and this one was no exception. The monetary squeeze turned out to be tighter and more effective than either ministers or policy makers expected. This was largely the result of the increase in real interest rates. For over a decade they had been negative. Between April 1979 and October 1981 real interest rates swung from minus 12 per cent to a positive real rate of almost 3 per cent. The potent combination of high real interest rates and a strong exchange rate represented very tight monetary conditions. The transition costs were also greater in scale than ministers expected, because the normal transition costs were aggravated by almost a generation's worth of industry change. This change had been artificially prevented by previous Conservative and Labour governments; it then took place rapidly. In effect, half a generation or more of necessary change that had been delayed was compressed into about three or four years. The temporary shock to demand also exposed the full deficiencies of UK product and employment markets.

The Retail Prices Index measure of inflation fell from an annual rate of 21.8 per cent in May 1980 to 3.7 per cent in May 1983. The disinflation was an outstanding success and laid the foundations for future sustained growth with manageably lower rates of inflation of around 3 to 5 per cent in the 1980s. Indeed, part of the recovery in output in 1981 and 1982 was a result of increased demand that arose from positive real balances effects that were the product of unexpected and steep falls in the rate of inflation, which halved between the spring of 1980 and the spring of 1981 to 11.7 per cent.

Monetarism was embodied in the Government's Medium Term Financial Strategy (MTFS), published in 1980. This set out a series of connected targets for monetary growth, government borrowing and inflation. There was a neat connection between each target and government spending, because the accounting counter-parties that made up £M3 included a direct link to the PSBR, which in turn reflected the level of spending and taxation.

The principal difficulty was that £M3 was not under the direct control of ministerial policy instruments. While high interest rates set by the Chancellor could reduce demand for money and choke off bank lending, in a measure of money that contained interest bearing deposit accounts, high real interest rates for the first time in a generation stimulated a portfolio adjustment. People parked large sums of money in bank accounts scored as part of £M3, to enjoy safety and high real interest rates on cash during a period of monetary squeezing and high commercial risks. The result was that instead of growth in the chosen measure of the money supply neatly and gradually falling, followed by a fall in inflation, the money supply measure being targeted continued to expand, while the rate of inflation fell as a result of the genuine squeeze in domestic monetary conditions and the rising exchange rate.

This was a cause of great embarrassment to Treasury ministers, who had to explain it and invited the effective taunt from Denis Healey that the Government had introduced a form of 'punk monetarism', along with irony from Ted Heath, who congratulated the Government on abandoning 'monetarist dogmatism'. The reason for this is that Milton Friedman's framework of monetary control to reduce gradually monetary growth and with it inflation, was worked up in the context of a measure of the money supply M1 in the US that did not at that time include interest-bearing savings accounts. In the UK when the first analytical work was done identifying a monetary indicator that offered a stable relationship with output and prices, it was £M3, which included interest-bearing deposit accounts. Given that policy worked indirectly on the demand for money through interest rates, any monetary target that included interest-bearing deposits was likely to yield some perverse and inconsistent results, although this would not in any way prevent such a policy from working.

These inconsistencies exposed a series of fundamental questions about the demand and control of money, direct and indirect controls on monetary growth, the information yielded by monetary indicators, the process of causation involved and the length and character of the monetary transmission mechanism. These were explored to an extent in a Green Paper on *Monetary Control* in

1980. It reads principally as a sort of study in ambiguity. By 1983 the settled position of the Treasury, set out in a seminal paper by Rachel Lomax that continued to be circulated internally within the Treasury for many years, was that inflation had come down, and an interest rate and exchange rate squeeze showed how it could be done. The difficult and fundamental questions elided by the Green Paper should be set aside, given their complexity, unless another serious inflation mistake happened.

The Government continued to set monetary targets, but changed their definition, experimented with new indictors and generally attached less importance to them, until in the 1985 Mansion House speech, Nigel Lawson, the Chancellor, and the original author of the MTFS, suspended the formal target for £M3, memorably saying that inflation would be judge and jury of monetary policy and inflation appeared to be firmly under control. This was the end of monetarism. As Harold Lever expressed it shortly before Nigel Lawson made that Mansion House speech: 'Nigel was clever enough to get himself into monetarism and he will be clever enough to get himself out of it'.

Chapter 6: The European Exchange Rate Mechanism

MONETARY POLICY IN PRACTICE had become wholly discretionary. The Chancellor, Nigel Lawson, however, sought an external anchor for monetary policy. Linking sterling to the Deutschmark had many merits. The Deutschmark was a well-managed currency, controlled by the most successful central bank, the Bundesbank, in the post-war years. Such a policy would be clear, easy to explain and its success would be easy to judge. But the Prime Minister did not like it. She preferred free exchange rates rather than fixed parity regimes. As a politician she may well have wanted to ensure that she never had to preside over an official devaluation of sterling for the perfectly understandable reason that is a very visible policy setback that carries severe political penalties for the government of the day. She certainly repeated the refrain that you cannot buck the market.

In practice, the Chancellor targeted the Deutschmark and exposed an import difficulty with exchange rate targets. There can be protracted periods when the measures necessary to maintain internal domestic monetary stability and the external anchor are inconsistent. Between 1986 and 1988 the economy was expanding above its trend rate of growth, asset prices and house prices were rising sharply, and the money supply and bank lending was expanding very rapidly. Much tighter domestic monetary conditions were needed, but the de facto objective of holding sterling at 3 Deutschmark to the pound meant that domestic interest rates were cut. This was needed to maintain the external objective, but it was the opposite of what any commonsense interpretation of the domestic economy would imply for monetary conditions.

This episode resulted in genuine tension between Chancellor Nigel Lawson and the Prime Minister, and introduced a frisson of irritation into what was otherwise a long-standing and harmonious political relationship. This irritation was about two issues in monetary policy. The first was the conduct of domestic monetary policy and the interpretation of the information yielded from indicators of monetary growth, principally £M3. This can be roughly summarised as the Prime Minister believing that very rapid monetary growth spelled trouble for the future in terms of higher inflation. It is probably misleading to attribute to it anything more sophisticated than that, but it was strongly felt on her part. The Chancellor was able to say that, in the past, rapid monetary growth had been a poor indicator of a build-up of genuine transaction balances in the economy and had therefore been a misleading guide to setting interest rates, and furthermore, inflation remained low during a period of sustained economic growth of around 3 per cent a year.

The leads and lags in monetary policy and the monetary transmission mechanism are variable. It appears that the transmission from monetary growth increased bank lending into house prices and then general inflation was much longer than either the Treasury or the Bank of England understood, with the result that monetary growth was translated into inflation of around 10 per cent in 1990. Revised economic data showed that the rate of economic growth was higher than initially reported and therefore even less plausibly sustainable. The sophisticated explanations offered by the Government Economic Service and the Bank of England were convoluted. The principal official explanation was that monetary growth was irrelevant or at least benign, because it represented a growth in bank balance sheets with growth in liabilities matched by growth in assets. This expansion of bank balance sheets was facilitating an inflation of asset prices that had few or no implications for the general rate of inflation. These sophisticated explanations turned out to be little better than gilt-edged tripe. The Prime Minister saw £M3 growth of 16 per cent for three years and saw inflation. What the officials in charge of the policy simply did not recognise was the obvious. This is an important example of Margaret Thatcher's judgement being vindicated in the face of that of nearly all her ministers and the civil service and the Bank of England who were supposed to advise her.

The second aspect to this episode was Margaret Thatcher's attitude to sterling entering the Exchange Rate Mechanism of the European Monetary System. The Chancellor, Nigel Lawson, was of the view that linking sterling to the Deutschmark was a reliable means of getting an effective monetary anchor and in effect piggy-backing on the stable demand for money in Germany and the exceptionally good record of the Bundesbank in controlling inflation. At a stroke it would avoid all the technical problems of interpreting M0, £M3 and bank lending and PSL2. Membership of the ERM would make an exchange rate target more credible, because it was part of a wider system of currencies where it would be easier to lock in a specified exchange rate objective.

Nigel Lawson also had growing reservations about the process of EU integration, the proposed European Social Charter and the work being done by a committee of experts led by Jacques Delors on the creation of a single European currency. The Chancellor felt that if sterling were in the ERM, aside from its perceived merits in terms of monetary management and control, it would make it easier for Britain to work against a series of undesirable and potentially very damaging developments. His view was that sterling's absence from the ERM was an irritant in the UK's relationship with other EC governments and made it more difficult to manage an already awkward set of relationships.

The European Exchange Rate Mechanism

Sir Geoffrey Howe, the Foreign Secretary, shared the Chancellor's view about the merits of the ERM as a monetary policy device, and wanted the UK to join for political reasons to strengthen the UK's commitment to European integration. The Foreign Office actively tried to get the Department of Employment to drop its opposition to the European Social Charter and the Social Action Programme of some 20 draft directives that accompanied it, while Nigel Lawson actively sought to encourage the Department of Employment to resist both.

Margaret Thatcher was opposed to sterling's participation in the ERM because of her dislike of fixed exchange rates and her perception that they limited domestic monetary discretion. She observed that, when the Treasury shadowed the Deutschmark and cut interest rates at time when domestic monetary conditions would suggest they should be tightened, far from anchoring inflation, the Deutschmark link could aggravate it. As she vividly expressed it at Question Time in the House of Commons, it was like pouring petrol on a bonfire.

In 1989, at the Madrid meeting of EC Heads of State and Government, the Foreign Secretary, Sir Geoffrey Howe, and Nigel Lawson, put a lot of pressure on the Prime Minister to agree that sterling would eventually enter the ERM when certain conditions were met. The truth is that for several years almost all her Cabinet with the notable exceptions of Nicholas Ridley and Kenneth Baker, were in favour of ERM entry. The only obstacle was the Prime Minister. Although, as Norman Fowler had pointed out at a lunch hosted by Lord Shawcross at the American bank J P Morgan, when this point was put to him by a meretriciously clever city economist, in his experience, 'the Prime Minister's opposition was a very substantial obstacle to something happening'.

During the last year of her administration in 1990, the Prime Minister was under sustained pressure from John Major, the Chancellor, and Douglas Hurd, the Foreign Secretary, to agree to sterling entering the ERM. They went about it in a tactful manner, going out of their way not to annoy her and persuaded her that, having agreed that sterling should go into the ERM at Madrid, not being in the ERM was making the management of the exchange rate very difficult, probably requiring interest rates to be higher than they needed to be. The foreign exchange markets had a tendency to respond to sterling negatively, particularly when there was any element of parliamentary controversy touching on the exchange rate at Prime Minister's Question Time, an event that was then played out twice a week. This, they argued, added to the political damage that arguments about the role of exchange rate were having on the reputation of the Prime Minister and the Government as a whole.

The British establishment supported the ERM. There were no dissenting voices in private among either Treasury ministers or senior or, indeed, junior Treasury officials. The Bank of England supported it as an article of faith, as did the whole of Whitehall led by the Foreign Office. Indeed, persuading the Prime Minister to join the ERM was John Major's great political triumph as Chancellor of the Exchequer. He had done something that Nigel Lawson and Geoffrey Howe had failed to do. The official Opposition led by Neil Kinnock supported it, as did the Liberal Democrats. The CBI and most business and financial leaders supported it, although within the City of London there were some significant voices of dissent, not least that of Tim Congdon. Sterling entered the ERM in October 1990.

In 1990 the principal issue in UK monetary policy was how to get inflation down and keep it down. It was acknowledged that getting inflation down from over 21 per cent to something between 3.5 and 5 per cent in the first part of the 1980s had been a huge achievement, but the Lawson boom returned inflation to 10 per cent. This was a huge disappointment. It required an exceptionally tight monetary squeeze, involving interest rates at 15 per cent to correct it, that Nigel Lawson put in place before he resigned as Chancellor. The argument for joining the ERM was that it should be an aid to lowering inflation and keeping it down. This meant that the chosen exchange rate should be sufficiently tight to lower domestic inflation and serve as a tough objective for the future. Moreover, Dutch and French experience of the ERM suggested that if an economy were to reap the full benefits of low inflation as a result of linking its currency to the DM, in terms of low interest rates, there should be no devaluation within the ERM. The exemplification of this was the franc fort policy pursued by President Mitterrand's Government in France after 1983.

Within 2 years the policy had collapsed in failure. In the same way that shadowing the Deutschmark illustrated how an economy might have to set interest rates that were too low to avoid inflation if an exchange rate target is to be maintained, the protracted recession in 1991 and 1992 demonstrated the reverse. After the sharp fall in output that resulted from Nigel Lawson's raising of interest rates to 15 per cent in 1989, tight monetary conditions had by 1992 reduced inflation. Yet in the summer of 1992, at roughly the bottom of the economic cycle – the data was later revised and now looks different to how it seemed at the time – sterling was falling against the Deutschmark. To maintain sterling's position in the ERM, interest rates would have to rise. This was plainly the last thing the British economy needed at that juncture. Worse, while sterling was falling against the Deutschmark, it was rising against the dollar and the overall trade-weighted sterling index was rising. To take discretionary action to tighten domestic monetary conditions was wholly inconsistent with what was necessary for the domestic economy. Part of the explanation for the rise in the Deutschmark related to measures being taken by the Bundesbank to contain the inflationary consequences of German unification, and its maladroit and damaging monetary union between East and West Germany. Despite the huge expense of foreign exchange reserves, the use of the Minimum Lending Rate and putting up interest rates to 15 per cent, the ERM commitment was abandoned. As the *Sun* memorably put it, commenting on the cost to taxpayers of the loss of foreign exchange reserves: 'Now we've all been screwed by the Cabinet'. Margaret Thatcher's assertion you cannot 'buck the market' was vindicated on this in the face of the judgement of her three Chancellors. Yet more than this, her judgement and instincts were vindicated on flexible exchange rates and the difficulties of both the ERM and a European Single Currency. In contrast, the whole of the British business, policy and political establishment and the overwhelming balance of the commentariat were wrong on the ERM. And a significant proportion of it was initially wrong on the euro as well.

Reducing British inflation in the early 1980s was a huge political achievement. It was the result of taking very difficult decisions and sticking with them and living with the high transition costs that were necessary to accomplish the policy. It was a personal achievement made possible by the Prime Minister. However, the intellectual, technical and institutional arrangements for the successful and orderly conduct of monetary policy, such as the creation of an operationally independent central bank, were not resolved. The return of double-digit inflation in 1990 was an immense disappointment. Higher than expected inflation created very awkward public expenditure problems for the Government through the impact that higher prices had on the indexation of benefits. It is a seminal episode of failure in monetary policy along with those of 1971 to 1973 and the conduct of monetary policy in years leading up to 2007. It was then compounded by the decision to take sterling into the ERM. Margaret Thatcher's reservation about the conduct of domestic monetary policy in the mid-1980s and her reluctance to agree to sterling entering the ERM offer interesting glimpses of the quality of her judgement, but do not diminish the policy failures involved. Despite the return to double-digit inflation, overall the objective of achieving significant disinflation was achieved.

The European Exchange Rate Mechanism

Chapter 7: The UK Industrial Relations Problem

THROUGHOUT THE 20TH CENTURY the labour market had been the Achilles heel of the economy.

The legal framework in 1979

BRITAIN'S TRADE UNION PROBLEM in 1979 was summarised by Lord Diplock in his judgement in the case of *Dupont Steels vs Sirs* 1980:

> 'The immunity from the law of tort over an area that has been much extended by the Acts of 1974 and 1976, is one that is intrinsically repugnant to anyone who has spent his life in the practice of the law or the administration of justice.
>
> Sharing those instincts, it was a conclusion that I myself reached with considerable reluctance, for given the existence of a trade dispute it involves granting to trade unions power, which has no other limits than their own self-restraint, to inflict by means that are contrary to the general law, untold harm to industrial enterprises unconcerned with the particular dispute, to employees of such enterprises, to members of the public and to the nation itself, so long as those in whom the control of the trade unions

is vested, honestly believe that to do so may assist it albeit in a minor way, in achieving its objectives in the dispute.'

The 1906 Trade Disputes Act exempted people organising industrial action, such as strikes, from the conventional law of tort. In practice it took the courts and the law out of industrial relations and greatly strengthened the position of unions and workers in relation to the owners and managers of businesses. When the Act was passed, even the strongest supporters of collectivism and trade union power such as the Webbs could not quite believe the extent of the immunity. Writing in the 1920 edition of their *History of Trade Unionism* that the Act 'explicitly declares without any qualification or exception, that no civil action shall be entertained against a trade union in respect of any wrongful act committed by or on behalf of the union; an extraordinary and unlimited immunity, however, great may be the damage caused and however unwarranted the act'. By the 1930s, trade union power was an obstacle that prevented wages from adjusting to changing economic circumstances. Lord Keynes argued in the Great Depression that, given that wages could not adjust because of what he called 'institutional' reasons, the price level needed to be increased through inflation to lower real wages and the cost of employment to reduce unemployment. In the Second World War, the Minister for Labour, Ernest Bevin, a former leader of the Transport and General Workers Union, pithily summarised what was wrong with British industrial relations, and explained low productivity in manufacturing, as the trouble is 'the buggers will not work'.

Social alienation and workplace cussedness

BY THE 1960S there was a significant literature cataloguing working class alienation and union obstruction in the workplace. Some of the best known contributors to it were writers and commentators who regarded themselves as firmly on the Left, such as Michael Shanks and Nicholas Davenport. An important part of the analysis was the belief that Britain had an entrenched class system. Society was hopelessly split with a 'them and us' syndrome, where the working class was alienated. The affluence of the 1950s and the 'never had it so good' Macmillan years in this analysis did not mitigate it, but compounded it. Workers felt that in an acquisitive society, they were being beaten by the rich, because they had capital, education and expertise. Nicholas Davenport wrote in *The Split Society* that:

> In the Macmillan epoch the sour, cynical, "browned-off" behaviour of the workers had in fact become pathological. This was evident from the number of frivolous strikes they indulged in. Railwaymen struck, because they could no longer get their hair cut by railway employees in railway time and on railway premises. Shipyard workers struck, because joiners and metal workers could not agree who should drill holes in aluminium sheets. Motor workers even struck because managements dared to alter the timing arrangements for the tea break.

Frivolous and destructive actions impeded business and industry. Writing in the *Observer* on 10 February 1963, Arthur Koestler commented that:

> 'In no other country has the national output been crippled on such frivolous and irresponsible grounds. In this oldest of all democracies class relations have become more bitter and trade union politics more undemocratic than in de Gaulle's France or Adenauer's Germany. The motivation behind it is neither communism, socialism, nor disenchantment nor enlightened self interest, but a mood of disenchanted cussedness.'

This behaviour in the workplace inspired a genre of cinema comedy exemplified by *I'm All Right Jack*, starring Peter Sellers. The conclusion among social democratic left-wing commentators was that there should be a reform of trade unions. In return for this reform that was intended to give union leaders greater power over their members, there would be union support for a prices and incomes policy. Union leaders would agree to control wage claims to facilitate full employment, while rising living standards would be generated by government-led investment, as part of the wider mixed economy, with inflation suppressed by controls on wages and prices.

As inflation became a more pressing problem in the 1960s, the Wilson Government resorted to a statutory prices and incomes policy. The unions would not accept it and even when their leaders tried to co-operate, unofficial action organised by local workplace shop stewards vitiated such support. There were increasing examples of so called 'wildcat' strikes, as well as a growing shop steward power base that was prepared to defy national union leaderships that were perceived as too close to supporting the Government, even a Labour Government's incomes policies.

The Donovan Report and the failure of In Place of Strife

THE RECOGNITION THAT THERE WAS SOMETHING FUNDAMENTALLY WRONG with British industrial relations is clear from the fact that a royal commission chaired by Lord Donovan was set up to look at the role of trade unions by Harold Wilson. It reported in 1968 and recommended the immunities should remain in place. The Labour Government, facing increasing union militancy and unofficial action, published instead a set of proposals in a White Paper, *In Place of Strife*, that proposed bringing trade union practice within a legal framework. Among its proposals were ballots before strikes, and the establishment of an Industrial Relations Board to compel parties to accept settlements in industrial disputes. The Prime Minister and Mrs Barbara Castle, the Secretary of State for Employment and Productivity, drafted it, but encountered intense opposition from trade union leaders and the TUC whose interests were formidably represented in the Cabinet by the Home Secretary, James Callaghan. The Prime Minister was eventually forced ignominiously to abandon his proposals to reform industrial relations. In practice, the defeat of *In Place of Strife* emboldened the unions from General Secretary to shop steward, and this invigorated audacity coincided with a wider international militancy among workers in the late 1960s.

The Industrial Relations Act, the miners, the three-day week, and Ted Heath

MUCH OF THE DETAILED AGENDA from *In Place of Strife* was taken up by the Conservative Party and put into legislation in the Industrial Relations Act 1971. It legislated for legally enforceable collective agreements, grievance procedures and an Industrial Relations Court to preside over this new framework of employment law. The TUC opposed the legislation root and branch.

In the late 1960s and early 1970s there was a radicalisation of trade unions and workers throughout Western Europe analogous to the radicalisation of students on university campuses. Part of this radicalisation was a greater willingness to defy the criminal law and to use violence as part of intimidatory picketing when pursuing industrial disputes. Moreover, as unions successfully defied Labour and Conservative governments, they became increasingly bold in pursuing their objectives.

Statutory incomes and pay policies exposed Labour and Conservative governments to direct challenges in a context where there was a series of large nationalised industries. Coal, steel, electricity and railways were covered by national collective agreements where for all practical purposes a government department stood behind the agreement as paymaster. This meant that an industrial dispute could swiftly become a direct challenge to the political and legal authority of the Government. This was particularly the case when Parliament passed legislation on incomes where workers striking in a nationalised industry dispute could force the Government to abandon enforcing legislation it had put on the statute book. The National Union of Mineworkers managed to do this twice within two years in 1972 and 1974. The second coal strike caused the Government to declare a state of emergency, order power cuts on a rotating basis and to restrict companies to a three-day working week to limit the use of electric power. The culmination of this was when the Prime Minister, Ted Heath invited the public to decide who governs Britain in an election called in February 1974, which he lost.

Labour's Social Contract, the Grunwick pickets and the Winter of Discontent

THE LABOUR GOVERNMENT AFTER 1974 with Michael Foot as Secretary of State for Employment set about resolving the unions' complaints. The statutory incomes policy went and was replaced by a 'Social Contract'. The Industrial Relations Act was repealed, full trade union immunities were restored, and their scope was effectively widened in two Trade Union and Labour Relations Acts.

In 1979 trade unions could not be sued, and as Lord Diplock explained in a judgement on the 1980 steel strike, a person engaged in pursuit of a trade dispute or trade union business was exempt from all civil law and the test as to what that business may be was wholly subjective. The use of intimidatory picketing had become commonplace. The Grunwick recognition dispute in Brent in London was notorious. Coach loads of pickets were organised from all over Britain to picket a small photographic processing company. It was *de rigueur* for Labour MPs and Labour Cabinet ministers to visit the picket. In a similar way, albeit without the same degree of violent intimidation, Blackwell's book shop in Oxford was subjected to a sustained picket.

By 1979, the Labour Governments of Harold Wilson and James Callaghan had given the unions what they wanted. This included a framework of law, a police service that was hesitant about applying normal criminal law procedures in relation to violent intimidation on picket lines, the abolition of incomes policy, full consultation and influence on most major areas of policy, and, over a period of 15 years, a huge increase in the role of the state and the level of taxation and public expenditure.

Yet the unions could not co-operate with the Labour Government. A key part of the Keynesian full employment consensus was that the unions should deliver pay restraint to control cost push inflation in return for the commitment to full employment, the controls on dividends and what was sometimes referred to as the social wage – the public spending on public services and Social Security benefits. In 1978 the public sector unions showed they could not co operate with this. Their rejection of the Labour government's pay terms led to a series of strikes that severely disrupted everyday public services, including the working of the hospitals, local authority refuse collection and municipal cemeteries. This is what lies behind the lurid memories of the 'Winter of Discontent'.

In the early part of 1979 it was clear that the unions would not work with Labour ministers any more reliably than they had worked with Conservative ministers. The social democratic agenda of European-style trade union reform envisaged by Michael Shanks, the journalist and economist, had failed. Indeed, in February 1975 one of the agenda's principal economic authors, Anthony Crosland, had made a speech to the Local Government Association telling them the local government spending party was over. By the 1970s, however, the agenda of the Labour National Executive Committee and much of the Parliamentary Labour Party had moved on from Croslandite social democracy to one of democratic socialism. This agenda was inspired by an Alternative Economic Strategy, re-mixing the mixed economy by making the public and nationalised sectors larger. There was also an increasing interest in more variant forms of public enterprise, including worker-led co-operatives as well as state investment funds such as the National Enterprise Board. The inspiration for much of this was more Tito's Yugoslavia rather than Helmut Schmidt's West Germany or Olaf

Palme's Sweden. The Social Democrats had been in charge for 15 years and they had comprehensively failed on their own terms. They did not halt Britain's relative economic decline and could not prevent a consistent perception of malaise when there was not a well-founded sense of economic, industrial and political crisis.

Trade Union law reform

THE THATCHER TRADE UNION REFORMS were not based on some clever agenda or a new political or social settlement. Instead they were a narrow set of limited and discrete measures. It was a Fabian approach that directly went to the heart of the problem: the immunity from tort for organisers of industrial action. It was supported by a macro-economic policy of disinflation. This recognised that inflation was a monetary phenomenon and that in the long term, rising wages were not a cause of rising prices, but a symptom. In order to reduce inflation, the post-war goal of full employment had to be abandoned, and it was. This transformed the balance of power between all employers and their workers.

The Thatcher approach to trade union reform was perfected by Norman Tebbit, the Secretary of State for Employment. It was a series of pieces of legislation that eroded the scope of the immunities that people organising trade disputes enjoyed from the law of tort. It removed the immunity from most forms of secondary strike action. And certain conditions had to be met before a union organising a strike could enjoy the conventional, albeit slightly narrowed immunity. This was principally the requirement that a properly conducted strike ballot had to be held. In addition, a number of measures were passed requiring trade union leaders to be elected and subject to the control and scrutiny of their membership.

A series of pieces of legislation was passed to remove legal sanction from the closed shop. This legislation was often unpopular with employers, as well as trade unions. Many large employers found it convenient to a agree on a closed shop with a particular union, and they vigorously opposed such legislation. This was an example of the way Margaret Thatcher decisively broke with the corporatism of the 1960s and 1970s. In many respects it was what *Marxism Today* called a guerrilla war. Margaret Thatcher avoided a direct general confrontation with unions. Avoiding direct conflict was made easier by the fact that the Government did not have an incomes policy enshrined in legislation.

The Government's wider supply-side agenda of promoting the use of the price mechanism and increasing competition in product and labour markets also played a significant part in limiting the role and power of the unions. The imposition of tough limits on the external financing requirement of the nationalised industries and privatisation of state owned industries was an important part of this process. More competition means that markets are more contested. More contested markets meant less scope for firms to maintain super-normal profits or monopoly rents. The removal of such monopoly rents removed the scope that firms had to share those rents with trade unions. In the context of a non-accommodating monetary policy, unions could not raise wages at the expense of profits within national income. All that results is that unions' success in raising wage rates results in employment falling.

Margaret Thatcher was wary of a conflict with the unions that could expose the Government to the kind of states of emergency that she had seen at first hand as Secretary of State for Education and Science in the Heath Cabinet between 1970 and 1974. Even before she became Prime Minister she showed she could compromise and hold back. Hence her willingness to accept the Clegg Commission's recommendations on public sector pay in 1979. In response to the Winter of Discontent the Callaghan Government commissioned Professor Hugh Clegg, who had served on the Donovan Royal Commission, to look into public sector pay. It amounted to a generous, and certainly expensive in public expenditure terms, agreement for public sector workers. Margaret Thatcher made it clear that in government the Conservatives would honour it, and she did. This played a part, along with the second oil shock, in making the first years of her Government very difficult.

The miners' strike

MARGARET THATCHER DID NOT SEEK A CONFLICT with the National Union of Mineworkers. The 1980 Coal Act guaranteed the National Coal Board £600 million a year of new capital investment. The demand for coal fell during the recession of the early 1980s, but the Coal Board continued to produce coal as if nothing had happened. The result was huge losses that could not be dealt with unless the Government was prepared to shut uneconomic pits. Pit closures would have provoked a miners' strike. In February 1981, at the first hint of a threatened miners' strike, Margaret Thatcher made the Secretary of State for Energy, David Howell, back down on a programme of pit closures. The Prime Minister was concerned that there were insufficient coal stocks at power stations for the Government to withstand a prolonged coal strike. It was a complete humiliation for Government. When Margaret Thatcher appointed Nigel Lawson Secretary of State for Energy in 1981, as he explains in his memoirs, her brief to him was succinct: 'Nigel, we mustn't have a coal strike'.

The central economic problem that the National Coal Board presented is best illustrated by its External Financing Limit (EFL) – the amount of money that the Government planned to inject in grants and loans to cover its annual losses. In 1981 the EFL of the National Coal Board was £1,117 million. This was more than the combined EFLs of British Steel and British Telecom. The Government was committed to spend a further £800 million on investment in new pits, while there was no market for much of the coal being produced. This resulted in total coal stocks at pitheads of 43 million tons, the highest level of coal stocks since the late 1960s.

Nigel Lawson recognised that there would eventually be a coal strike. He ensured that coal was moved from the pitheads to the electricity generating power stations, where it was needed. In addition, he ensured that there were substantial stocks of the things needed to generate electricity besides coal. These included chemicals and materials such as oxygen necessary for the combustion process. Some of these have a short life and arrangements were made to ensure that power stations could be supplied by helicopters if necessary. David Howell had started this process of building up coal stocks at power stations, but in a deliberately low-key manner. This was because ministers were concerned that the miners might consider such action as provocative and could have resulted in a strike. The Secretary of State for Employment, James Prior, considered Lawson's proposals to build up the stocks on a scale that would be visibly apparent as dangerously provocative.

These coal stocks were not really accumulated as part of some Machiavellian political planning by Margaret Thatcher and her minister. Instead they arose from the inevitable; that is, uneconomic coal pits engaged in raising productivity and producing as much coal as the management and unions could manage. The unity of purpose between the National Coal Board management and the National Union of Mineworkers could not be exaggerated. It resulted in one thing: a lot of coal that nobody wanted to buy. That is why coal stocks were high in 1984. The question was whether the people who legally owned it, and wanted to buy it and use it, would be able to do so. The two principal nationalised industries involved were the National Coal Board and the Central Electricity Generating Board. The question was whether they would be able to use and move around the coal that had already been mined in the normal way. In 1972 and 1974 Arthur Scargill and his flying pickets had been ruthless and skilful at preventing coal stocks and other materials being used to generate electricity. On 10 February 1972, 2,000 picketing miners forced the police to shut the Saltley Gate Coke Depot in Birmingham. In the early 1970s the police in effect acquiesced in the criminal law being broken. In the mid

1980s, despite criminal violence and intimation by NUM pickets, they did not. The interesting thing for historians will be to examine what the official papers say about this. What role did the Government and the Prime Minister have in directly changing the attitude of the police? Nigel Lawson's memoirs suggest that the Home Secretary Leon Britton encouraged the police to enforce the law.

The Government was right to prepare for a coal strike. The mines were uneconomic and the NUM would not accept that pits would have to be closed where it cost more to produce the coal than anyone was prepared to pay for it. The only arrangement the NUM appeared to be content with was massive subsidies to keep uneconomic pits open until, as Arthur Scargill put it, the last piece of coal was removed, combined with a huge programme of capital investment in new pits to produce further unwanted coal.

Arthur Scargill was the leader of the Yorkshire miners who had organised the flying pickets that forced the police to withdraw at Saltley Depot. He was a hero of 1970s trade union militancy; the man who brought down Ted Heath's Conservative Government in 1974. Scargill saw violence as a political weapon and was prepared to use it against the Government and other unions that did not co-operate with him. He told the *New Left Review*, for example, that the Transport and General Workers Union 'had a contractual arrangement with the working class that if they didn't honour, we'd make sure physically that they did. For we would have thrown their lorries and everything else into the dyke'. Arthur Scargill was elected President of the NUM with the support of 70 per cent of miners in a ballot in 1982. In his first presidential address to the NUM he set out his fundamental position: 'every trade unionist has to be determined to defy the law and to render it ineffective'. Arthur Scargill was a dynamic, reckless Marxist, who had played a large part in bringing down one Conservative Government and thought he could do so again.

In 1984 the National Union of Mineworkers, without the full support of the union membership and without a national ballot, started a coal strike. The strike was started in the spring when the summer months meant a protracted period when consumption of coal would be at its lowest. The NUM strike was not supported in Nottinghamshire, where the pits produced at full capacity. This meant that the winter of 1984-85 came and went with little fall in the coal stocks at power stations. The strike ended on 5 March 1985.

The strike was reckless folly for the miners. As Nigel Lawson's memoirs explain, it was costly and damaging for the country. It revived memories of the 'Who Governs Britain?' debate of the 1970s. While opinion polls showed that the public was opposed to Scargill, the support for the Conservative Party plummeted in the polls. The strike provoked a sharp fall in the sterling exchange rate in 1985 that required a strict tightening in domestic monetary conditions. Recorded industrial output stagnated and the rate of GDP growth fell sharply. The coal strike resulted in large public expenditure costs. The coal industry and its two principal customers – steel that used one-fifth of the output, and electricity that used three-quarters of it – were all nationalised. The biggest cost was burning oil in power stations rather than coal and there were additional costs from hiring trucks to transport coal from working pits to power stations. In 1984-85 the public expenditure planning total was exceeded by £3.5 billion, two-thirds of which was attributable to the miners' strike. The strike added £2.75 billion to the Public Sector Borrowing Requirement, that year.

The defeat of the miners' strike and Arthur Scargill's unconstitutional challenge was a central event in the history of the Thatcher Government. It is of major constitutional importance. As Nigel Lawson commented: 'Just as the victory in the Falklands War exorcised the humiliation of Suez, so the eventual defeat of the NUM etched in the public mind the end of militant trade unionism which had wrecked the economy and twice played a major part in driving elected governments from office – James Callaghan's in the aftermath of the Winter of Discontent in 1979 no less than Edward

Heath's in 1974'. Economically, it was also important because it ensured that the normal disciplines of the market economy such as a hard budget constraint and the need to make profits would be extended to coal. Until then coal and the miners were the strongest bastion of non-market production.

The strike was caused by the reckless behaviour of Arthur Scargill and a significant proportion of the membership of the NUM. It remains at the heart of much of the folk memory and continuing hostility to Margaret Thatcher. It was a very bitter event. During the most difficult periods during the violent strike she remained determined and used language that made that political determination clear. On one occasion she told the Conservative 1922 Committee that the hardcore Scargillite acolytes were 'the enemy within'. Much of the folk memory of the coal strike is kept alive by BBC programmes such as Radio 4's *Woman's Hour* and plays on Radio 4 exploring the Kellingley Colliery sit-in by the wives of miners led by Mrs Ann Scargill. These explore and celebrate the genuine courage and fortitude of the miners' wives during the coal strike. Less is done to recall the courage of the working miners and the violence and intimidation that they and their families faced. Part of the hostility to Margaret Thatcher is that when the miners went on strike, her government was not destroyed, unlike Ted Heath's Government in 1974. Margaret Thatcher did not court trouble with the unions; her instinct was to try and avoid it if she could. She did not want to be Ted Heath Mark II. The coal strike is the exemplar of how her opponents sought to provoke trouble with her. The economic and financial problems of the coal industry could not have been resolved in a more emollient manner because the NUM and Arthur Scargill made that impossible.

Ending the Dock Labour Scheme

MARGARET THATCHER REMAINED WARY AND CAUTIOUS of national strikes right to the end of her days in government. For 40 years the Dock Labour Scheme had given unions an effective veto over working arrangements and pay in Britain's docks and emasculated the country's greatest natural harbours and historic ports. Every major and minor port and harbour in 1947 from Liverpool to Fowey was listed. A new and inconvenient port, Felixstowe, had been started and flourished because it was outside of the Dock Labour Scheme and the Dock Work Regulation Act. The case for legislative reform was overwhelming. The Prime Minister was very reluctant to act because she did not want to risk a national dock strike. Much to the irritation of her true believing parliamentary and junior ministerial supporters, she would not agree to tackle it. Only in the spring of 1989 did the Prime Minister agree to legislate to reform the Dock Labour Scheme. And right until the last moment – the weekend before the announcement – it was made clear that she reserved her position. In the months and weeks leading up to it, she made it clear to backbench MPs pressing her to do it that she was 'sorry to disappoint them'. She finally agreed to it with one of her most experienced ministers in charge of the legislation and handling the strike that followed. Norman Fowler was one of Margaret Thatcher's most effective ministers and had the benefit of having once been the Minister of Transport. The role of Norman Fowler in the abolition of the Dock Labour Scheme is a reminder that Margaret Thatcher achieved a lot, but she did not do it all on her own. She had the benefit of some remarkably able and interesting ministers. They included Nigel Lawson, Geoffrey Howe, Norman Tebbit, Kenneth Baker, Kenneth Clarke, Nicholas Ridley and Lord Young.

The sea change in strikes and days lost through industrial disputes

POOR INDUSTRIAL RELATIONS AND STRIKES distinguished British industrial relations in the 1960s and 1970s. By the 1990s it was clear that the position had been transformed. There were fewer strikes than at any point since the records were first collected in 1891. The average number of strikes between 1990 and 1995 was a tenth of what it had been between 1975 and 1979. In 1979, 29 million working days were lost through strikes. In 1995, 415,000 working days were lost as a result of 231 stoppages of work. In the 1970s, an average of 12.9 million working days was lost each year as a result of strike action. Trade union membership fell by around two-fifths from 13.3 million in 1979 to 8 million in 1995. It continued to fall in the 21st century to 7.5 million in 2005. In the private sector, the number of employees covered by a collective agreement fell significantly and identifiable trade union wages premiums – the trade union wage mark-up – fell. A profound process of de-unionisation took place in the final 20 years of the 20th century. In 1979 53 per cent of workers were union members; by the late 1990s this had fallen to 30 per cent. In 1980, around 70 per cent of employees' wages were set by collective agreements. By the mid-1990s this had fallen sharply to less than 45 per cent

Margaret Thatcher's reform of trade union law and the wider programme of labour market reform transformed industrial relations and ended the labour market acting as the UK's economic weakness. It was in many respects contingent. Union militancy had gone so far that it had dissipated its popular base of democratic support. In 1979, the country was ready for a government that would begin to do the obvious, whether unions liked it or not. The NUM under Arthur Scargill's leadership went out of its way to challenge the government over pit closures, not just demanding jobs guaranteed for life, but jobs in every pit guaranteed for two or three generations. It was an extraordinary piece of reckless provocation. And a piece of provocation based on an audacious calculation that their pickets would again override the Government and the taxpayer at large. This reckless piece of syndicalism gave Margaret Thatcher the opportunity to show that the unions could be undone. That a government could say no, mean it, and survive. Arthur Scargill was foolish and miscalculated. His crucial failure was to underestimate the determination and willpower of the Prime Minister. She was different from other post-war occupants of Downing Street. Trade unionists such as Scargill illustrate why the necessary reforms that Margaret Thatcher's Government carried out could not be done in a more emollient manner. The emollient ideas of the people such as Michael Shanks had failed in the 1960s. That is why Harold Wilson and Barbara Castle published *In Place of Strife*. The social compact and full accommodation of the trade unions on industrial relations law and much of economic and social policy by Labour governments in the 1970s had descended into the chaos of the Winter of Discontent. Something needed to change radically and Margaret Thatcher accomplished that change.

Chapter 8: Profits and the Crisis of British Capitalism

THE UK ECONOMY IN THE 20TH CENTURY suffered from a series of structural weaknesses. These contributed to a pronounced relative economic decline. Much of this relative decline was probably inevitable and an artefact of being the first industrial nation. Yet there were structural weaknesses that were evident regardless of the state of the economic cycle, which resulted from policy decisions made by successive governments. The labour market was inflexible in terms of wage setting, investment was low, the capital stock antiquated, productivity was poor and the rate of return on investment was weak. These were long-standing matters, and they were evident in the 1950s. Nationalisation carried out in the 1940s, rather than helping to remedy these weaknesses, appeared to compound them. By 1960 it was clear that the UK had entered into a noticeable relative decline compared to other comparable mixed economies in Western Europe. The West German economic miracle based on Ludwig Erhard's social market showed that a devastated Germany could easily outperform the UK economically and financially. Sweden, with a social democratic model based on privately owned enterprise generating tax revenue to finance generous public services, offered a model of affluence and egalitarian progress. And France and Italy were examples of rapid growth where living standards were catching up. An essential part of the UK's problem was the weakness of its private sector in general and the manufacturing sector in particular. British manufacturers found it difficult to innovate in a commercially successful manner and to export in contested markets.

This process of noticeable relative decline developed into a genuine crisis of British capitalism in the late 1960s and mid-1970s. The economists who best grasped the fundamental character of it were usually drawn from the Marxian tradition. Marxist economists tended to explore the structural characteristics of economies. They have a habit of looking at the inherent conflicts of economic interests and the contradictions that market economies and political institutions exhibit. A Marxist economist therefore can see a crisis of capitalism when there is one. And it was often the aristocratic, Marxist economists based in Oxbridge colleges such as Andrew Glyn at Corpus Christi College, Oxford, who led the way in explaining these matters. Andrew Glyn and Bob Sutcliffe in *British Capitalism Workers and the Profits Squeeze*, published in 1972, provided a cogent account of the way a series of long-standing structural problems became a genuine crisis of capitalism.

Glyn and Sutcliffe's book starts with a crisp summary of the conditions necessary for market economies to function and what happens if they are not in place:

'Capitalism is a system of production dependent on private profit. It cannot operate without sufficient profits; they are the incentive which drives capitalists to invest, and they provide much of the finance for investment. A decline in profits, therefore, forces some firms out of existence and by reducing investment in others, prevents living standards from rising. In these ways it sets up forces which threaten the survival of the capitalist system'.

They went on to assert:

'Our argument in this book is that British capitalism has suffered such a dramatic decline in profitability that it is now literally fighting for survival. This crisis has developed because of mounting demands from the working-classes for faster economic growth in living standards has coincided

with growing competition between capitalist countries. This competition, apparent in conflicts over trade and exchange rates, has prevented British capitalism from simply accommodating successful wage demands by pushing up prices correspondingly.'

This acute profits squeeze did not just happen in the late 1960s. It arose out of a combination of several things. Inflation, pay policies and poor industrial relations wreaked havoc with incentives and productivity. A series of policies from Selective Employment Tax, the structure of capital allowances and corporation tax, to policies determining the geographical location of industrial investment, blunted the normal incentives present in a market economy. The attitude of Labour governments in the 1960s was that risk-bearing capital and returns on equity were of little importance. Anthony Crosland, a former economics don at Trinity College, Oxford and the chief theoretician of the moderate Gaitskellite social democratic wing of the Labour Party, regarded ownership of industry through joint stock equity as being of little importance. In *The Conservative Enemy* Crosland argued that, in modern corporations, managers were more concerned about good public and labour relations than profits. The result was that managements did not seek profits as consistently or as ruthlessly as they once did. If policy overrode and blunted market incentives and reduced the rate of return on capital, there would be few significant consequences. Moreover, if public sector finance was available to increase investment through the nationalised industries, the establishment of public enterprises and industrial subsidies to support innovation and reorganisation of privately owned firms, the implication was that the rate of return on capital was of little significance.

Margaret Thatcher understood the role of profit in capitalism and the role of incentives in markets. Her chancellors systematically took measures that restored financial incentives to work and investment. The three biggest changes she made that reversed the profits crisis were:

❑ Abandoning prices and incomes policies;

- Delivering a successful process of disinflation;
- The radical reform of the trade union law.

Just as it was the Marxist economists who noticed the gravity of the British crisis of capitalism in the early 1970s, so in the 1980s it was economists who were rooted in the Marxian tradition who understood the fundamental changes that Margaret Thatcher's governments were bringing about. Indeed, Andrew Glyn complained to an adviser to the Conservative Party, Walter Eltis, the economics don at Exeter College, Oxford, that he was very worried that the progress being made in reviving profits meant that capitalism was recovering. Likewise, it was articles in *Marxism Today* that catalogued the radical reorganisation of the British economy. Many naïve mainstream economists mistook bankruptcy and the uncomfortable, but inevitable and overdue, change as evidence of some sort of failure. The contributors to *Marxism Today* recognised it for what it was: a successful, albeit from their perspective ruthless, process of Schumpeterian creative destruction. The contributors to *Marxism Today* understood that uncomfortable changes were being made that would clear the way for future growth and the accumulation of capital.

Chapter 9: Nationalised Industries, the Mixed Economy and Privatisation

BY 1990, WHEN MARGARET THATCHER LEFT DOWNING STREET, the mixed economy was dead. Today, it is not just dead, but increasingly forgotten. In 1979 the mixed economy was an entrenched fact of everyday life. Much of British political debate aired in the columns of the *Financial Times* and the *Economist* was about how best to run the mixed economy. It was about how to recruit the heads of nationalised industries and how to improve their management. All the basic industries – gas, electricity, steel and transport – were nationalised. Fifteen per cent of the workforce and 20 per cent of the capital stock was applied to producing 10 per cent of the country's national income. They were badly managed, and subject to confused objectives that resulted from the political process that determined all the major decisions that touched their businesses. They had been established in the 1940s without much of a clear plan of how they would work and several government White Papers had failed to establish an effective modus operandi for them, resulting in the last major White Paper, *The Nationalised*

Industries, published by the Labour Government in 1978 reading like a catalogue of errors.

There were important and complex matters that had to be sorted out, among them the need for a hard budget line to protect the taxpayer, protecting consumers from the opportunity presented to governments to extract revenue from the monopoly profits arising from natural monopolies and ensuring that environmental externalities were properly addressed. These were normally fudged in private. Matters were usually decided in accordance with the line of least resistance: over-manning, huge investment programmes in wrong places, pay and working conditions that were not matched by productivity, and prices to consumers that did not cover the costs of providing the goods and services or the costs of the nationalised industries.

In 1979 it was an article of faith among British economic commentators that the nationalised industries and the mixed economy were here to stay. Who would want to buy them, was the usual refrain. The only example of a successful denationalisation that economic lecturers could cite was Volkswagen, a child of the West German economic miracle.

The achievement of establishing financial discipline in the nationalised industries and returning most of them to profit and the private sector was remarkable. It was also unexpected. *The Right Approach to the Economy* and the 1979 Conservative manifesto said little about denationalisation. The 1987 manifesto, although offering a rolling programme of asset sales, was guarded about the future of coal. Yet privatisation was without doubt a massive political achievement. There was a large element of learning on the job. It would be wrong to suggest that it was carried out in an economically optimal manner. There was a genuine learning process involved. Selling off whole industries without enough competitive challenge was a mistake. It partly reflected the tension between seeking to maximise the proceeds of a sale, by in effect offering investors a stream of monopoly profits, and trying to create better market structures and regulation.

Until privatisation, the tensions and conflicts of interest between government departments, the Treasury, the taxpayer, the consumer and the public at large were not made explicit. Instead they were glossed over in private. The Government regulated the environment, yet it owned industries that had the greatest potential to despoil it. This led to a tension between the Government as a regulator and as the ultimate paymaster. The Government could set external financing limits on monopoly providers, who could pass them on to consumers, like any other monopolist. By exposing these issues, privatisation has resulted in better frameworks of regulation, environmental protection and consumer protection. The framework of regulation based on the RPI plus or minus model was an important innovation in utility regulation. It certainly was not perfect, but it was a big improvement. Moreover, the process of privatisation exposed costs and misleading policy advice from officials and nationalised industry managers. The best example is the cost of nuclear power in electricity generation. For 40 years this was presented as expensive in terms of capital investment, but cheap overall as a source of energy. It turned out that the decommissioning costs were never properly scored and minister after minister had been misled. Far from being cheap, nuclear was expensive.

The programme of denationalisation removed some 45 major businesses – about two-thirds of the nationalised sector – from the public sector. It involved transferring over 900,000 employees from state to private employment. Industries that were costing the taxpayer £50 million a week in subsidies in 1979 were by the early 1990s contributing £2 billion a year to the Exchequer in corporation taxes on profits. The users of former public-owned utilities benefited from significant reductions in the real costs of phones, gas and electricity. In the years that followed the privatisation of BT, prices fell by 27 per cent and domestic gas prices fell by over 12 per cent. There were huge improvements in the service provided both to domestic consumers and to businesses. In 1979 it was illegal to use a phone unless it was bought from the nationalised monopoly. Customers often had to wait for a new phone to be installed and internal long-distance 'trunk' calls often could not be made because all the phone lines connecting major cities were often overburdened and just offered the caller the engaged tone.

In 1979 the nationalised industries accounted for a tenth of GDP, a seventh of total investment in the economy and around a tenth of the Retail Prices Index. They employed one and a half million people and dominated the transport, energy, communications and shipbuilding sectors of the economy. Their total return on capital employed was low. Their record on prices, productivity and customer satisfaction was poor. Dismantling the nationalised industries and the mixed economy was one of the most radical changes that Margaret Thatcher wrought.

Margaret Thatcher: The economics of creative destruction

Chapter 10: A Capital-Owning Democracy

MARGRET THATCHER WAS A CONSERVATIVE POLITICIAN. She had an agenda that was about creating wealth and opportunity for people. She passionately believed in private property rights and giving as many people as possible the opportunity of starting a business and rewarding those who were successful. This meant creating the economic and policy conditions where people could accumulate savings and capital and where existing accumulations of private property were not disturbed or threatened by policies such as estate duty, wealth taxes or heavy property taxes such as the domestic rate burden exhibited in the mid-1970s. Margaret Thatcher's challenge in 1975 was to obtain political consent for her agenda. Moreover, her agenda was one that was perceived by the British political establishment to be either 'all that we have tried to get away from', or completely impossible to win consent for.

Margaret Thatcher set out to widen the possession of directly owned private wealth. She promoted private home ownership, the accumulation of private pensions, and wider share ownership. Councils were compelled to sell tenants their homes at a significant discount. The tax system was changed to subsidise firms rewarding their employees with bonuses that were taken in the form of shares in the business and held for five years. As well as private occupational pensions provided by companies, personal pensions enjoying similar tax relief to the company-based arrangements were established. An important objective of the programme of denationalisation was wider share ownership. The ubiquitous character Sid, used to advertise the share issues of privatisations, led to many smaller savers happily buying apparently undervalued shares. Although, many people 'stagged' them in the classic manner of the City of London, privatisation widened share ownership and encouraged much greater interest in financial markets, savings and investment in general. Millions of people who would never have thought of owning shares directly or accumulating nest eggs of capital began to do so. The introduction of Personal Equity Plans (Peps) and Tax Exemption Special Saving Accounts (Tessas) created a ration of saving each year that could be put aside without any liability to income tax, or in the case of shares held in Peps, income and capital gains taxes. The incentive to save and accumulate a long-term capital sum was increased by the ending of investment income surcharge on savings income. In 1979 one adult in 20 owned shares in a company; by the 1990s almost one in three did so. The development of Peps and Tessas mitigated the double taxation of savings exhibited by any income system and in effect gave savers a cash sum that could be put aside each year that received expenditure tax treatment.

Home ownership will always be associated with Margaret Thatcher. Owner occupation rose from 56 per cent to 69 per cent between 1979 and 1990. During her period in power, six million households bought their homes, and 1.4 million people bought their council home under the Right to Buy scheme introduced in 1980. Home ownership was encouraged by Mortgage Interest Relief at Source or MIRAS, that had been introduced by Roy Jenkins in 1969. It assisted borrowers by giving them tax relief on their interest payments. The tax allowance was raised by Sir Geoffrey Howe in the 1983 Budget from £25,000 to £30,000. Home ownership was supported by the deregulation of credit markets. Restrictive guidelines on building society lending were ended in

1979, the Reserve Asset Ratio applied to banks was ended in 1981 and the building societies cartel collapsed in 1986. Competition in mortgage lending increased in the second half of the 1980s with specialist, often American, mortgage lenders entering the UK market. The effect of the old cartel arrangement was to lower mortgage rates below their market level and to limit the supply of mortgages that were rationed through a queuing system. An enhanced tax subsidy, the ending of borrowing restrictions and the accommodation of pent-up demand for credit for house purchase were a recipe for an explosion of lending.

Given the constraints on housing supply, arising out of the planning controls put in place by the Attlee Labour Government in the 1940s, it was a recipe for relative house price inflation. House prices doubled between 1985 and 1989 and rose in real terms by 70 per cent. This explosion of credit was at the heart of the Lawson boom. The effect of higher house prices on the economy was made greater because of the expansion of home ownership. This had effects on other borrowing through hire purchase, often connected with moving house, and on household consumption more generally through the wealth effects arising out of the increase in value of a household's principal asset. The increased borrowing operated to reduce the savings ratio, because borrowing is netted off against household saving, with the result that the savings ratio collapsed, falling from over 14 per cent in 1980 to less than 4.5 per cent at the peak of the Lawson boom. The incentives created to encourage people to opt out of the state second pension – SERPS – and into personal pensions and the marketing of personal pensions as a whole encouraged people to sometimes opt out of employer-based final salary occupational pension schemes that they would have been better off sticking to. This was part of the mis-selling scandal. Some of the people who were encouraged to buy shares and invest in them through Peps felt that, after charges and even with the tax relief, the returns were often disappointing. And there were moments when the responsibilities of servicing a mortgage on a property that could not be sold because of negative equity during the first part of the 1990s could appear a curse. While more people accumulated early capital and savings, the distribution of wealth widened and richer households accumulated housing and financial assets at a faster rate than households in the middle. However, this wider dispersion in the distribution of wealth and the evident problems should not obscure the broader picture of a society where many more people owned property and accumulated more capital through a wider range of investment and savings instruments.

Margaret Thatcher succeeded in creating a society where more people owned assets, possessed savings and directly owned shares. As the Prime Minister told Conservative parliamentary candidates ahead of the 1987 General Election, 'capital is now something that ordinary people have; before the only capital they knew about was *The Forsyte Saga* on the BBC on Sunday nights'. Politically, it was an astute and an effective strategy. By 1990 a large part of the British electorate had a direct personal stake in a well-functioning market economy. Millions of people owned shares in former nationalised industries, owned their own homes, possessed savings, were the beneficiaries of occupational and personal pension funds and had mortgage liabilities. This created a society where left of centre parties could not nationalise private firms without proper compensation to shareholders or tax savings and income from investment in a punitive manner. By 1986, the Labour Party had to start to adjust to social and economic realities that politically constrained it. Trade unions with members who have to pay the mortgage each month and have some cash savings and investments, have members who are much more reluctant to take strike action than the culture of the asset-free Labour movement that Michael Shanks analysed in the late 1950s.

Chapter 11: 1976: the End of the Keynesian Consensus

THE POST-WAR FULL EMPLOYMENT CONSENSUS can be easily set out.

In the 1941 Budget speech Sir Kingsley Wood announced that the wartime National Government accepted that the purpose of the Budget was not just to set and fund expenditure but to use the budget balance to manage the economy. In the 1944 Employment White Paper, the Government committed itself to maintaining full employment. The Chancellor made short-term decisions to manage demand so that there would always be enough aggregate monetary demand in the economy to ensure full employment. Government spending and deficits would be used to stimulate demand if necessary. When demand was too great and there was inflation, borrowing would be cut, spending would be cut and taxes would rise. There was a reluctance to use monetary policy in general and to raise interest rates in particular. This was because monetary policy was perceived as irrelevant and interest rates should be kept very low to encourage investment that was assumed to increase employment. Government borrowing and public debt was assumed to be costless as part of the doctrine of functional finance developed by Abba Lerner. If there was inflation, it was assumed that workers would not notice it and would not demand higher wages. Should there be inflation, it would best be contained by wage restraint, and wage restraint was more likely to be accepted by workers and unions if prices, profits and dividends were also directly controlled.

The policy approach was agreed by the Churchill wartime coalition Government. All three political parties signed up to in the 1941 Budget and the 1944 Employment White Paper. In the 1950s the *Economist* called it Butskellism because both Labour (Gaitskell) and Conservative (Butler) Chancellors applied the same policies. As inflation rose and the resulting fall in international competitiveness progressively weakened the balance of payments, steadily greater control over wages and prices were advocated. This became what Robert Skidelsky called 'authoritarian Keynesianism'. Lord Keynes himself was a Liberal and an admirer of Hayek's book *The Road to Serfdom*. In practice, however, he was content with extensive government control over things such as foreign exchange, foreign travel and investment. Over time, instead of being counter-cyclical, active demand management policies amplified the economic cycle.

The failure of Keynesian economics

BY THE 1950S THERE WAS A PRONOUNCED STOP-GO CYCLE and by 1970 at each peak and trough of the cycle, inflation and unemployment were higher. As the Conservative Chancellor of the Exchequer, Ian Macleod, who died five weeks after taking office, noted in July 1970, unemployment was at its highest level since 1940, and wages were at the highest level for 20 years, with prices not far behind. The final full-scale Keynesian reflation of the British economy happened in 1972. Unemployment had reached a million and Ted Heath's Government 'went for growth' and tried to contain the rising inflation embedded in the economy, by legislation that prescribed a prices and incomes policy in law.

By the end of Heath's Conservative Government, everything that could go wrong had gone wrong. Inflation was rising, sterling was falling, unemployment was rising and the Government's incomes policy had all but collapsed in a state of criminal violence and public disorder. The initial reaction of the minority Labour Government that took office in February 1974 was to pretend there were no problems, and then seek a majority in the further election that took place in October 1974. The following year was a period of extraordinary financial and economic crisis. The Government did nothing about it, because in effect it faced a further electoral test in the form of the June 1975 referendum to decide whether Britain would remain within the EEC. After that, the Labour Cabinet began to set about trying to address the country's severe economic crisis that had been put on hold for over a year. It was another iteration of a non-statutory pay policy announced by the Prime Minister Harold Wilson at the traditional Durham Miners' Gala, an event of much significance in the Labour movement at that time. In this speech the Prime Minister, originally an economist by training and a former economics don at University College, Oxford, used a startling expression: 'one man's pay increase is another man's ticket to the dole queue'. This turned on its head the conventional Keynesian refrain that wages had nothing to do with unemployment.

In February 1976, the White Paper *Public Expenditure to 1979-80* set out in graphic terms the UK's long-term public spending problem. Its introduction still offers one of the best practical expositions of the structural problems created by public spending. Later that year the recently elected leader of the Labour Party, James Callaghan, told the Labour Party Conference that:

'We used to think that you could spend your way out of a recession, and increase employment by cutting taxes and boosting government spending. I tell you in all candour that that option no longer exists, and that in so far as it ever did exist, it only worked on each occasion since the war by injecting a bigger dose of inflation into the economy, followed by a higher level of unemployment as the next step. Higher inflation followed by higher unemployment. We have just escaped from the highest rate of

1976: the End of the Keynesian Consensus

inflation this country has known; we have not yet escaped from the consequences: high unemployment.'

This passage, apparently drafted by Mr Callaghan's son-in-law Peter Jay, the economics editor of the *Times*, was a landmark in the end of the British Keynesian system of economic policy. A further sterling crisis that month resulted in the Government approaching the IMF for a loan. The IMF imposed conditions to the loan. Among them were further cuts in planned public spending. Unemployment was rising sharply, compared to its post-war full employment level. Instead of using fiscal policy to hold it down, policy was tightened to address the structural budget deficit and the balance of payments position. As part of the IMF conditions, monetary targets were set for domestic credit expansion. 1976 was the year when the post-war Keynesian consensus actually fell apart.

The counter-revolution in political economy

THE KEYNESIAN WELFARE STATE was subject to a frontal intellectual assault in the 1970s. Lord Keynes's *General Theory of Employment Income and Money* and the intellectual revolution that it had brought about had for some time been subject to a sustained technical challenge from monetarist economists in America, such as Milton Friedman. In the mid-1970s there was a much broader challenge to his legacy of political economy. Two Oxford economists wrote a series of high profile articles in the *Sunday Times* in 1976 that became a book, *Britain's Economic Problem: Too Few Producers*. This book, although presented in the conventional Keynesian framework, argued that an over-expanded state could not sustain full employment and living standards through public expenditure and that Britain had a public expenditure problem analogous to that of the 18th century *ancien régime* in France before the Revolution. In *The Future That Doesn't Work: Social Democracy's Failures in Britain*, edited by Emmett Tyrell, a group of American and British journalists and academics argued that 'well intentioned programmes can lead to economic disaster.' Peter Jay's, chapter, 'Englanditis', argued that in Britain and in western Europe the social democratic mixed welfare economy was not working and would have to be replaced by an alternative. He wrote:

'Any alternative must either seek to work through the basic principles of liberal economics, acknowledging the role of prices in balancing supply and demand, or try to override them, presumably substituting either commands or spontaneous altruism by all economic units'.

This counter-revolution in political economy did not go wholly unchallenged. In 1978 the London correspondent of the *Washington Post*, Bernard Nossiter, published *Britain – A Future that Works*. Nossiter argued that 1970s Britain pointed the way to an attractive post-industrial world, where production of manufactured goods was allowed to pass to Far Eastern economies, that would concentrate on high value-added technological exports and would give greater emphasis to leisure, even if that meant slower growth in living standards. Nossiter is a good example of the sort of pastoral apologist that Sir Nicholas Henderson referred to in his valedictory dispatch on British economic and political decline sent in March 1979. The fundamental weaknesses in Nossiter's analysis included: the assumption that the British people were happy to trade income for leisure; that the trade unions were demonstrating that they 'have come to understand there are limits they must impose on their own power – union members see that their well-being now requires a measure of union restraint'; and that workers in old uncompetitive heavy manufacturing and extractive industries would acquiesce in their gradual rationalisation and restructuring. A few months after the publication of Bernard Nossiter's book, Britain experienced the full expression of irresponsible trade union power, militancy and intimidation. The steel and coal strikes in the 1980s were to demonstrate that the unions were not prepared to cooperate with the orderly restructuring of their industries. The unions were happy to agree to nationalised industry investment plans that created new plants and then vigorously oppose the closure of uneconomic old

1976: the End of the Keynesian Consensus

plants and mines that had always been central to the original investment plan.

To use a funereal metaphor, Margaret Thatcher was not the Prime Minister who buried the Keynesian consensus, but she was a pallbearer at the funeral, who had offered a withering commentary on its demise and turned out to be the executrix of the will. In the process she became the political standard bearer for a broader intellectual revolution. She had founded the Centre for Policy Studies with Sir Keith Joseph. Speeches delivered both by Sir Keith and Margaret Thatcher advanced a clear direction of travel that broke decisively with the post-war consensus. And that critique and direction of travel was mapped out, as the Keynesian system fell apart, while she led the Conservative Opposition. It represented a move away from discretionary counter-cyclical demand management policies towards a more rules-based approach to monetary, fiscal policy and the public finances and the greater use of markets and the price mechanism.

The direction of travel changed in terms of public spending control, a monetary approach to inflation, a reduced role for the state, a reduction in marginal tax rates, greater incentives and a fundamentally different view of political economy – 'some of our children can grow taller than others'. This transformed the political agenda, and broke the consensus. These were all laid down before Margaret Thatcher entered Downing Street. In 1979 Margaret Thatcher took power as the political standard bearer of a counter-revolution in political economy.

The 1981 Budget and the 364 economists who did not like it

IN MARCH 1981, at the trough of a deep recession, Sir Geoffrey Howe tightened fiscal policy. Taxes were raised by £4 billion to deal with the structural budget deficit. Income and capital gains tax thresholds were frozen. The Public Sector Borrowing Requirement was £10.5 billion in 1981-82 compared to the £7.5 billion implied in the MTFS. The fiscal tightening was accompanied by a relaxation in monetary conditions and a lower exchange rate that provided the economy with a powerful monetary stimulus. It was the complete repudiation of the standard Keynesian policy prescription. 364 economists wrote to the *Times*, arguing that there was no basis in theory or supporting evidence that the Government would be able to bring inflation permanently under control, that the policy measures would deepen the recession, and that without a change of policy there could be no sustained recovery. As it happened, the letter almost coincided with the start of the recovery in output that began in the second quarter of 1981. Thereafter the UK economy enjoyed a sustained expansion in output that averaged around 3 per cent for some eight years or more. The economists who wrote the letter represented mainstream academic opinion. The interesting thing is not that they wrote the letter or that they turned out to be wrong, but that they were relatively quiet in 1976. The real watershed was Denis Healey's White Paper cutting public expenditure when unemployment was rising, the speech of Mr Callaghan to the Labour Party Conference, and the IMF conditions for the loan.

Margaret Thatcher's 11 years in power were the working out of a 'philosophy' mapped out in Opposition. It lead to connected policies stabilising inflation, improving incentives and the working of the supply side, a monetary squeeze, discretionary reductions in government spending and borrowing, and changing the character of the tax system to reduce its distortion and deadweight costs. These policies and their broad objectives cohered, but it is a mistake to exaggerate their consistency and neat ideological coherence. They were more of a rough working-out of things than a neat or elegant ideological template. They were practical policy responses to problems.

1976: the End of the Keynesian Consensus

Chapter 12: North Sea Oil

THE DISCOVERY OF OIL IN THE NORTH SEA was regarded as an unqualified blessing yielding simple economic benefits or rents to any political community fortunate enough to own it. This is the general perception of most discoveries of significant natural resources. In fact, an unexpected increase in the production of a single item that has a significant impact on the traded goods sector and the balance of payments is more complicated. What made North Sea oil production economic was a huge increase in oil prices in 1973. This increased the real resource cost of using oil. The UK economy, along with the other advanced economies in the OECD, was a user and consumer of oil. A huge increase in the real resource cost of such an important item was therefore damaging for economic welfare, whether the oil was produced in Saudi Arabia or in the North Sea.

Moreover, moving from being a net importer of oil to being a significant exporter of oil in a relatively short period had implications for the balance of payments and the exchange rate. North Sea oil transformed the current account deficit into a significant structural surplus during the first half of the 1980s. The UK went from producing no oil in 1975 to self-sufficiency in 1980 and exporting roughly 60 per cent more than the UK used in 1983. This inevitably resulted in a rise in the external value of sterling. Given that markets are forward looking, this started in the late 1970s. A higher exchange rate had negative implications for British manufacturing exporters and firms operating at home in markets contested by foreign suppliers. The inevitable result would be a higher exchange rate, fewer non-oil exports and more imports, with domestic UK businesses being crowded out by foreign competition. This process has been explored in a substantial body of international economic literature examining comparable events, such as the discovery of gold in 19th century Australia and the so-called 'Dutch Disease' following the development of natural gas in Netherlands in the 1960s.

The Treasury and the Bank of England understood the potential problem. In 1977, when the pound started to recover after the sterling crisis the previous year, the Treasury tried to cap its value. This was done partly to accumulate foreign exchange reserves, but really to protect the competiveness of UK manufacturing industry. It was swiftly abandoned because it would have required a massive expansion of the UK money supply to absorb the foreign demand for sterling that could not have been effectively sterilised — offset — by the Bank of England to prevent a matching increase in domestic liquidity. An increase in liquidity on that scale would aggravate UK inflation that remained high, despite a very brief fall in the late 1970s.

Adjusting to the impact of North Sea oil would have been difficult for any economy. Yet it posed particular problems for the UK. Successful adjustment with least pain or disruption requires prices, product and labour markets to be flexible. In the UK economy in 1979, price signals and most forms of incentives were blunted by structural rigidities: trade union power, a complex tax system, and a plethora of controls and rules. Among the rules were exchange rate controls which, if retained in 1979, would have aggravated the increase in sterling's value by preventing people from taking money abroad in a straightforward way. The increase in oil production and the rise in the exchange rate meant a change in relative prices; because the UK economy was so sluggish at responding to relative price changes, the change required had to be very large. In an economy where business and normal management had been distorted for years by prices and incomes policy, poor industrial relations practices, anachronistic working arrangements, government bail-out of bankrupt companies such as British Leyland, and the periodic short-term assistance of exchange rate devaluation, the inevitable adjustment was going to be very uncomfortable. And it was. Between 1979 and 1982 North Sea oil and gas output rose by 72 per cent and manufacturing output shrank by 15.75 per cent. The balance of payments recorded a large current account surplus that reached £6 billion in 1981, matched by a large deficit on the capital account as financial institutions invested abroad.

There is a charge levelled against Margaret Thatcher's Government that it 'squandered North Sea oil'. The charge is at best economically naïve, given that it implies its development was wholly benign and trouble-free, which it plainly was not. James Callaghan apparently went around saying that the government that won the 1979 election would be very powerful because of the discretion that North Sea oil revenues would give it. This view did not properly take account of the problem of the exchange rate and the Dutch Disease issue. Mr Callaghan published a White Paper, *The Challenge of North Sea Oil* (Cmnd. 7143) in March 1978, that set out what a Labour Government would do. The stronger balance of payments position would be used to expand demand to return the economy to full employment – a classic Keynesian demand stimulus, with the external trade position financed by oil revenue. This expansion of demand was to be supported by an increase in UK international competiveness, brought about by a prices and incomes policy to control prices and keep the costs of production down. Industrial efficiency was to be improved through further government intervention funded by oil. There would be enhanced Selective Assistance to the regions and a greater role for the National Enterprise Board. Industrial development would have been planned, with government, unions and employers planning the economy sector by sector. It was to have been firmly tripartite. The implementation of the Bullock Report was identified in the White Paper on oil as the key innovation to promote industrial democracy, so that the benefits of new investment and machinery and new techniques were realised. Tax revenue and royalties were to be used to finance cuts in personal income tax. There was to be a strong emphasis on public sector investment, regional industrial assistance and investment in the nationalised industries. It singled out the importance of public investment in communications and docks and harbours. Interestingly, the White Paper rejected the suggestion of setting up a North Sea Oil Fund on the grounds that it would 'either largely be cosmetic or have the effect of undesirably separating the decisions that will have to be taken. With the Government having one set of priorities for fund revenue and another for the use of its programmes, there would be a risk of confusion and misallocation of national resources'.

The White Paper contained one sentence at the bottom of page eight that touched on the exchange rate implications for the British economy and the adjustment that was inevitable. 'The market rate for sterling may be stronger than would otherwise be justified by the underlying competitive position of United Kingdom industry.' Hence the emphasis placed on control of inflation and improvements in the cost base. Yet the policies that the North Sea Oil White Paper relied on would fail and would have aggravated the problems of the UK economy. The necessary changes and reform were simply not on the agenda. The Bullock Report would have extended some of the worst features of the Dock Labour Scheme to industry as a whole. Higher spending on the nationalised industries would have aggravated the problem of low rates of return on UK industrial investment. Enhanced Selective Assistance and investment by the National Enterprise Board would have run up against all the previous problems of picking winners and deadweight costs. Investing in the docks without the abolition of the Dock Labour Scheme would have been costly and the investment would not have yielded satisfactory returns, given the way the scheme worked in practice. The centrepiece of the policy was a Keynesian reflation of the economy, with the balance of payments protected by oil and inflation held in check by an incomes policy. This seemed plausible to Labour ministers in March 1978, but such a notion collapsed with the Winter of Discontent within a year.

North Sea Oil

Chapter 13: The Public Sector Borrowing Requirement Becomes the Public Sector Debt Repayment

ANY DISCUSSION OF NORTH SEA OIL swiftly moves into the territory of the UK public finances in the 1980s. Throughout most of the period from 1945, governments ran budget deficits over the economic cycle, the notable exception was at the end of the 1960s, when as part of the IMF terms accompanying the 1967 devaluation, there was a brief period of surplus. Deficit financing was central to the neo-Keynesian doctrine of functional finance.

The Medium Term Financial Strategy

THE THATCHER ADMINISTRATIONS transformed this position. The most important innovation made to fiscal policy was the introduction of the Medium Term Financial Strategy (MTFS). This was first published in the 1980 Budget and projected illustrative falls in monetary growth, real government expenditure and the Public

Sector Borrowing Requirement (PSBR), which was projected to fall from 4.75 per cent of GDP in 1979-80 to 1.5 per cent in 1983-84. It was never fulfilled in any mechanical sense and many economic commentators pointed out that it often appeared to be honoured in the breach rather than the observance. Yet the fiscal targets and broad direction of travel were achieved and taken a stage further when the objective of balancing the budget over the economic cycle was announced. The PSBR, for example, fell to 3.1 per cent of GDP in 1983-84, roughly double that projected in the original MTFS in 1980, but the projections set out in the 1984 Budget were more than achieved. The PSBR was illustrated to fall from 3.25 per cent of GDP in 1983-84 to 1.75 per cent in 1988-89. In the event there was a surplus from 1987-88, and in 1988-89 the Public Sector Debt Repayment (PSDR) was 3.1 per cent of GDP. At the peak of the economic cycle, there were five years of surpluses that directly contributed to reducing the public debt to GDP ratio to 27 per cent from 47 per cent in 1980-81.

This transformation in the public finances came about as a result of a series of connected discretionary policy measures, including the changes made to curb public expenditure growth, such as ending the link between unemployment benefits and previous earnings. There was tight control of public sector pay and the imposition of strict running costs on central government departments in Whitehall, which lowered public sector employment. Public expenditure on investment and housing was limited. The imposition of strict external financing requirements on the nationalised industries, the reduction of state subsidies to industry, and receipts from the sale of nationalised industries and other state assets, such as local authority owned council houses, that were scored as negative public expenditure, all contributed. These contained public expenditure pressures and helped to reduce the level of public expenditure as a ratio of GDP to 38 per cent.

The tax burden and marginal tax rates

THE AGGREGATE, NON-OIL TAX BURDEN was increased from 34 per cent in 1979 to 37 per cent of GDP in 1990-91, having peaked at almost 38 per cent in 1981-82. The balance of taxation was changed. The VAT tax base was extended and the rate was almost doubled from 8 per cent to 15 per cent. The threshold for paying income tax was raised and marginal income tax rates were reduced. The basic rate of income tax fell from 33 per cent to 25 per cent and an objective was set to reduce it to 20 per cent. The top rate of tax fell from 83 per cent to 40 per cent. Investment income surcharge was abolished and a limited element of tax expenditure treatment was introduced to mitigate the double taxation of savings income, with the establishment of Peps and Tessas. The proportion of tax revenue accounted for by VAT doubled, rising from 7 per cent in 1978-79 to 14 per cent in 1989-90. Income tax receipts fell as a proportion of total tax revenue from around third to just over a quarter.

There was much debate about the scale of the cuts in marginal income tax rates in the second half of the 1980s. The system was simplified and the top rate of income tax was dramatically reduced. The strong growth in cash receipts and the rise in the non-oil tax burden shows that the Thatcher governments did not cut tax, but merely remitted part of the fiscal drag that means the effective tax burden rises in normal circumstances, given that the tax system is only partially indexed for prices and not for increases in earnings. This meant that taxes went up unless the Government took discretionary measures to remit the fiscal drag. This was partly done.

The changes to VAT, income tax, National Insurance and Corporation Tax amounted to a formidable record of tax reform. The tax base was widened, tax rates were lowered and the balance of taxation was shifted away from income and capital towards expenditure. The tax system became more neutral and less biased against saving and employment. There were fewer reliefs and distortions.

The Public Sector Borrowing Requirement Becomes the Public Sector Debt Repayment

Tax policy became an important part of micro-economic policy directed at improving the supply performance of the economy.

North Sea oil made an important contribution to this. Revenues from oil taxation and royalties peaked in 1985 yielding over 8 per cent of total government receipts. For about eight years North Sea oil added something between 0.75 percent and 2.5 per cent of GDP to total general government receipts. It made a significant contribution to containing the PSBR in the difficult period of structural adjustment in the first half of the 1980s and to the reduction in the stock of government debt. Revenue from oil was used to fulfil the Government's objectives. These were to improve labour market incentives as part of a wider policy of improving the working of product and labour markets and to restore long-term discipline to the public finances.

Chapter 14: Margaret Thatcher and the City of London: What She Did Not Do

MARGARET THATCHER WILL ALWAYS BE ASSOCIATED with the City of London.

In Opposition she argued that criticism of capital markets, the stock exchange and financial institutions was not about attacking rich people and privilege, but the way normal people saved through insurance policies, occupational pensions and unit trusts. Her governments took a series of measures that strengthened London's position as an international financial centre and widened share ownership. The three major policies were the abolition of foreign exchange controls in 1979, a series of measures that have gone down in history as the 'Big Bang' and the programme of government asset sales as part of denationalisation, and the ending of the mixed economy that widened share ownership.

The Big Bang emerged from an agreement between the Government and the London Stock Exchange in 1983 to end fixed minimum commissions and to open the Stock Exchange to outside investment. A similar set of institutional changes had taken place in New York in the mid-1970s. Fixed minimum commissions had been introduced by the Stock Exchange in 1912 to enforce the rules introduced two years before, separating out the roles of stock jobbers from that of stockbrokers. Its main effect was to increase the costs of buying and selling shares for large institutional investors such as pension funds and insurance companies. Stockbrokers could not compete in terms of price so they differentiated themselves through the quality of their service, and their research in particular. It was this non-price competition that encouraged the City lunches with all the paraphernalia of directors' and partners' dining rooms. In practice, a series of privileged relationships protected from price competition were ended. Among them was the anomalous position of the Government Gilt Broker at Pember and Boyle. This function was taken inside the Bank of England. The issuing of gilt-edged securities and trading arrangements for them were changed. The UK government bond market was remodelled to conform to the institutional arrangements of the US Treasury market, with auctions and primary dealers. These were all worthwhile and improved the functioning of the markets involved.

The main effect was to eliminate the oligopoly position of existing firms of stockbrokers, removing a reliable stream of income from them that would normally be regarded as a monopoly rent. In practice, something rather odd happened. Part of the changes allowed non-stock market firms to invest in and indeed buy firms of stockbrokers outright. This was intended to increase the capital base of London's stockbrokers which were perceived as undercapitalised compared to their international competitors, particularly those based in New York, such as Merrill Lynch. This change in stock market rules led to a boom in stockbroking assets. The stockbrokers were partnerships and they sold out to the American, Japanese, French, English and Scottish banks for large sums of money. The result was that a generation of partners coming up for retirement in around 1987 enjoyed handsome payments for their equity in the partnerships. As the competition for a limited number of firms increased in 1987, partners were offered golden handcuffs to prevent them from retiring and removing their skills and valuable human capital from their firms. This was all very strange because banks were choosing to pay a premium to acquire firms that had once enjoyed a monopoly rent that was about to be eliminated. The human capital they were acquiring and appeared so anxious to retain was obsolete and unfamiliar to trading in a market structure where there was price competition. This all happened in the last year of a long bull market in equities, which meant that, as well as paying for a stream on oligopoly profits when the oligopoly was about to be broken open, there was a premium reflecting the fact that the oligopoly had enjoyed additional super-normal profits in the financial years leading up to the valuations used for the sales of their partnerships. The new owners of stockbrokers then set about expanding their sales, investment and research teams to position themselves in the new market structure. This led to a frenzied round of recruitment and golden hellos. This was the origins of the 'loads of money' Thatcher epoch in the City. The fall in equity prices in October 1987 brought the merry-go-round to an abrupt halt.

These innovations brought significant changes to the culture of London's gilt and equity markets. There was greater professionalism and much less lunching. The Big Bang was accompanied by a series of pieces of legislation that ended the self-regulation of securities trading in London and placed it on a statutory footing. There were high profile examples of fraud prosecution and a new office for serious fraud investigation was set up. Insider dealing was dealt with toughly in the Guinness case in 1986. It is quite mistaken to view the process of change associated with the Big Bang as some form of deregulation. In effect, it was the application of competition law and the opening of a monopolistic market that previously had restrictive trade practices that had been tolerated by the competition authorities.

The Big Bang was a striking episode, and privatisation and wider share ownership were important British financial and social developments, but the modern international role of London as a financial centre had little to do with Margaret Thatcher. She may have understood its importance, celebrated it and tried to support it, but it was not her creation.

London's international role

WHAT MAKES LONDON UNUSUAL as a financial centre is its international role. A distinguishing feature of the City of London is the extraordinary range of wholesale and specialist financial markets. They include commodity markets such as the London bullion market and the London Metal Exchange, specialist markets in services such as Lloyd's insurance market and the Baltic Shipping Market, as well as the world's largest foreign exchange market. These wholesale financial markets had nothing to do with the Big Bang and Margaret Thatcher. Indeed, some of them, such as the Lloyds insurance market, were the beneficiaries of discretionary tax and other policies that could be traced back to the Attlee Labour Government and Sir Stafford Cripps, the Labour Chancellor of the Exchequer in the 1940s.

The most significant event in the evolution of London as a modern international financial centre was the development of the Eurocurrency markets and the Eurobond market in the 1960s. As a financial centre based in a declining economy in the 1960s and 1970s, London was saved by the Kennedy Administration. London's traditional financial role was that of being the money and capital market for the world's first industrial economy and the financial centre of a great colonial empire where trade was based on sterling, a reserve currency once buttressed by the international gold standard. In 1960 most of the international business done in London was legacy business. It reflected historical associations. The rationale for maintaining those historical relationships was evaporating fast. Sterling as a reserve currency was in its death throes, as relatively high inflation and devaluation administered a steady dose of euthanasia to its reserve status. The financial needs of the British economy and its declining industry would offer little staying power to a genuine international financial centre. There was little reason in 1960 to think that in 40 or 50 years' time London would be the world's principal international financial centre and would flourish as never before.

The seeds of this potential future success, however, were there. The eurodollar money markets developed in the 1950s. This was not so much because of any deliberate policy as a response to particular circumstances and the incentives generated by a particular framework of regulation. There was an accumulation of dollars in London. This resulted from US government spending on defending Europe, Marshall Aid money, the counterpart to the West German export miracle – Volkswagen Beetles had to be paid for in dollars, and the USSR's reluctance to deposit its dollar receipts from the sales of precious metals and oil in New York. A key driver that ensured that dollars were placed in banks outside the US was that minimum reserve requirements did not apply to dollar deposits outside the US. Banks could make more money out of a foreign deposit and in turn could pay more to attract deposits. The latter factor was reinforced when interest rate ceilings on deposit accounts, the notorious regulation Q, got in the way of American banks paying realistic rates when inflation pushed market interest rates higher in the 1960s.

The Kennedy Administration, however, managed to engineer a first-order policy mistake. 'Camelot' brought the best and the brightest to the White House. It was the Kennedy Administration that introduced Keynesian demand management properly into American economic policy. One of the ambitions of the Administration was to engineer an increase in the economy's level of investment and at the same time to protect the US dollar against outflows on the capital account. It was decided that it would be helpful to lower the long-term rate of interest in order to increase the capital stock. This was to be achieved by the US Treasury Department concentrating its borrowing at the short end of the maturity spectrum and staying out of the long end. In addition, the Yankee bond market used by foreign borrowers was effectively closed by the imposition of an interest equalisation tax, intended to stop American investors from buying bonds issued by foreign borrowers to buttress the capital account and the value of the dollar. The Treasury Secretary, Douglas Dillon, told Congress that the tax would divert security issues from the US and that it was equivalent to raising long-term interest rates by 1 per cent. The policy was a failure: the yield curve did not adjust in the intended manner and investment did not increase. But the policy did result in a permanent legacy. This brief interlude in the 1960s enabled London to establish a business issuing bonds denominated in dollars that happened to be held outside the US.

The way was led by SG Warburg Co in 1963 with a bond issued for Autostrada, a company that wanted to borrow in the US market, but was effectively prevented from doing so by the US Treasury Department's policy. So instead they issued a bond in London and tapped the euro-dollar market in Europe. Issuers of so-called euro-dollar bonds swiftly appreciated the fact that a dollar bond issue in London was cheaper and easier to carry out than a bond issued in New York. This was because in London the issuer did not have to comply with the onerous regulatory requirements of the Securities and Exchange Commission. It was cheaper and easier to issue dollar bonds in London free of such regulation.

By the 1970s London's international currency and bond markets, the so-called eurodollar and Eurobond markets, were well established. A Labour Party document, *The City – A Socialist Approach*, described the position accurately in 1982. Saying the operations of international banks had:

'grown enormously in the last 15 years. For example, the total deposits taken by American banks the UK in 1967 were £3,300 million. By the end of 1981 they had reached £77,800 million. This increase reflects the attractions of London as a financial sector and the enormous growth *in what are termed 'Eurocurrency' markets in currencies, mainly dollars, outside their country of origin. These combined effects have made Britain, and the City in particular, the centre of international banking'.*

In 1981 lending to non-residents and foreign currency lending to residents in the UK was $559 billion. In comparison, in the next highest ranked country in the world, the US, international lending was $214 billion. In terms of assets held in the UK, in 1981, overseas banks dwarfed all other financial sectors. Overseas bank assets were £255 billion, representing over 40 per cent of all assets held in the UK. Total clearing bank and building society assets, for example, were £150 million. The Big Bang did not create London's modern international money and bond markets.

The curious thing is that when most financial commentators are asked to account for London's current success while referring to light touch regulation, they often tend to emphasise the role of the Big Bang in 1986. The Big Bang was about the much needed modernisation of Britain's domestic markets, the gilt market and the London stock market. It had little to do with London's international markets. What it did do was to expose the conceit that London financiers, inhabiting its merchant banks, stockbrokers, stockjobbers and discount houses were uniquely talented repositories of financial expertise. The Big Bang swiftly demonstrated that the institutions at the heart of London's domestic securities markets did not possess the capital, the appetite for risk, or the expertise to compete in an open and competitive market.

They were rapidly bought by foreign banks, sometimes paying a premium for the brand and for the skills and experience of the people working them. They frequently choose to tie in the partners and employees to the businesses through golden handcuffs. At the time, this was a something of a puzzle. Foreign banks were paying over the odds for valuations of earnings based on an oligopoly that was about to be broken open. Earnings that, moreover, reflected the super-normal profits generated during a bull market. The human capital that was being acquired was likely to be obsolete or at least significantly depreciated, because the market structure it related to had been transformed from a form of monopoly to relatively open competition. Within less than a generation these great names were totally forgotten. Rowe and Pitman, Hill, Samuel & Co, Morgan Grenfell, Vickers da Costa and De Zote and Bevan are now names of interest only to financial historians.

Chapter 15: The National Health Service, Housing and the Welfare State

MARGARET THATCHER TROD VERY CAREFULLY when it came to the principal expenditure programmes of the welfare state. There were significant reforms that contained future growth in spending on Social Security transfer payments, such as the decision to uprate the basic state pension by the RPI instead of by prices or earnings, changes to the state second pension and ending the earnings-related link between unemployment benefit and previous employment. Yet the overall record is one where the welfare state was maintained, even extended, and placed on a financially sustainable footing. There was no destruction of the welfare state.

Health

IN SEPTEMBER 1982 THE THEN CABINET THINK-TANK, the Central Policy Review Staff, produced a report looking at future public expenditure trends. Among other things canvassed was the use of private insurance for part of the provision of the NHS. The report resulted in a Cabinet row and was leaked to the *Economist*. The

Prime Minister swiftly made it clear that the 'NHS is safe in our hands'. And so it turned out to be. Total NHS spending rose by 32 per cent in real terms between 1979 and 1990. In-patient waiting times fell by about 8 per cent. Between 1979 and 1990 the number of hip replacements rose by 54 per cent, cataract operations by 139 per cent and coronary artery bypasses by 356 per cent. The number of GPs increased by 22 per cent between 1978 and 1990. In 1990 there were 370 patients as an average on a GP's list, a fall of 16 per cent compared to 1978. In 1990 there were 17,000 more hospital doctors and dentists than in 1978. The number of nurses and midwives rose by 69,000. Doctors' pay rose by 46 per cent and nurses' pay rose by 43 per cent in real terms. The coverage of immunisation and breast cancer and cervical screening programmes was extended. The Government responded effectively to the new public health challenge presented by Aids, spending over £73 million on public health campaigns.

The White Paper *Working for Patients* published in January 1989 set out the proposal for the development of an internal market within the NHS. Its purpose was to create a quasi-market structure with shadow prices to improve the efficiency of the NHS. While the Labour Party taunted the Prime Minister with the charge that this amounted to privatisation, it was no such thing. Not least, because the Chancellor Nigel Lawson regarded health spending as 'sui generis'. He recognised that a tax-financed health service was an effective way of providing good health care and controlling its cost more effectively than insurance-based systems. The Chancellor would liked to have seen more use of charging for things, such as prescriptions, but the Prime Minister would have none of it. As Nigel Lawson ruefully noted in his memoirs, the proportion of NHS spending financed by charges was lower in the 1980s than in the 1950s when real incomes were lower.

Spending on personal social services also rose. The number of local authority day centre places for older people rose by 43 per cent. The number of local authority day home care workers 'home helps,' for older people, rose by 29 per cent. The number of meals on wheels served and provided by local authorities rose by 13 per cent, and the number of people in residential care settings rose from 152,900 to 235,500. The number of places in hostels for people with learning disabilities rose by 16 per cent. Day training centre places for learning disabled people rose by a third and the number of council staff helping them in homes and hostels almost doubled. Moreover, there were significant improvements in the quality and inspection of these services for older and disabled people. The classic Florence Nightingale geriatric NHS hospital ward was largely replaced by more appropriate nursing and residential care home provision.

Education

EDUCATION SPENDING PER PUPIL rose by 50 per cent in real terms. Education spending fell as a ratio of GDP from a peak of about 6.5 per cent in 1975-76 to 4.5 per cent in 1990. This was the result of falling pupil numbers in the 5 to 9 age cohort. In real terms, spending on books and equipment rose by over a third between 1978 and 1990 and capital spending per pupil rose by 15 per cent. The number of young people going to university increased by a third between 1979 and 1990. The proportion of 18 to 19 year olds going to university doubled from one in eight to one in five. Spending on higher education rose by 9 per cent in real terms. The UK spent more on higher education as a proportion of GDP than almost any major European country, largely because the government paid the tuition fees for students.

In the 1970s there was growing controversy about educational standards, which resulted in the Labour Prime Minister James Callaghan initiating a great debate on education. Margaret Thatcher's governments responded to continuing concern about educational standards with three significant changes to school education. Testing at 16 was changed, with the Certificate of Secondary Education

(CSE) and the O-level examinations being merged into one exam. A national curriculum was introduced with a framework of testing. Schools were given greater discretion from local education authority control, with the introduction of delegated budgets and an increased role for parents and governing bodies. The broad framework of non-selective secondary education remained in place, but new initiatives such as city technology colleges were introduced.

Social Security

SPENDING ON SOCIAL SECURITY rose by 31.8 per cent in real terms. Spending on benefits for the long-term sick and disabled rose by over 50 per cent in real terms. Norman Fowler's White Paper *Reform of Social Security*, published in 1985 and implemented in 1988, simplified Social Security benefits and concentrated them on those in greatest need. It introduced a new benefit, Family Credit, that extended help given to low-income working households with children and replaced Family Income Supplement (FIS). After 1986 through programmes, such as Restart, the administration of the unemployment benefit condition that a claimant should be seeking work was significantly tightened, partly in response to criticism from the Public Accounts Committee. A new Actively Seeking Work Test was introduced. The generosity of the state second pension, the State Earnings Related Pension Scheme (SERPS), was reduced. Instead of being based on the 20 best years of earnings it was changed to the lifetime average, and its rate of accrual was reduced from 25 per cent of earnings to 20 per cent of earnings. These and other technical changes to SERPS would yield substantial savings to future governments.

Pensioner incomes rose significantly in the 1980s. Pensioner households increasingly benefited from occupational pension funds and income from savings and investments. Between 1979 and 1988 gross pensioner incomes rose in real terms by 36 per cent, income from savings by 110 percent, income from occupational pension funds by 99 per cent, with income from benefits increasing by 14 per cent. Occupational pensions and the new personal pensions introduced by the 1988 Social Security reforms enjoyed significant tax relief, and paid no tax on their dividend incomes.

Housing

DURING THE FIRST EIGHT DECADES OF THE 20TH CENTURY the number of council houses in Britain had steadily grown. By 1979 over a third of the total housing stock was in the hands of social landlords. Margaret Thatcher threw that secular trend into reverse. The Conservative manifesto in 1979 pledged to give council house tenants the 'legal right to buy their homes.' The 1980 Housing Act gave council tenants who had lived in their homes for three years the right to buy them with a discount of 33 per cent on the market value for a house and at a discount of 40 per cent for a flat. During the passage of the legislation Michael Heseltine, the Secretary of State for the Environment, said it would 'lay the foundations for one of the most important social revolutions this century.' It gave 5 million people the right to buy, and some 1.5 million people exercised that right. The combination of council house sales and technical changes to local authority financial regulations that prevented receipts from council housing being spent as they arose until the council's debt had been repaid, together with the restricted permissions to borrow from the Public Works Loan Board, reduced the proportion of the housing stock owned by local authorities. Council house sales rose significantly from around £750 million in 1979 to over £5.5 billion in 1989. By 1985 local authorities had accumulated receipts from sales amounting to £6 billion, without any obligation to repay their accumulated debts. The Chancellor, Nigel Lawson, was concerned that this stock of liquidity could enable councils to increase their spending at any time, driving, as he saw it, a coach and horses through the Government's public spending and borrowing policies; and, moreover, increasing spending in a particular year from a source of non-recurrent finance that could exert pressure on the Government to increase its annual grant to local authorities. In many ways the episode provides an example of the necessary but much resented Treasury control that has to be asserted over local government, given that two-thirds of its funding comes from central government. Most public sector capital investment in social housing in the 1980s was channelled through the Housing Finance Corporation to housing associations. This further eroded the dominance of the mid-20th century council estate, because a significant proportion of the stock of registered social landlords came in the form of shared ownership and a less dense concentration of social housing. Nigel Lawson was a strong supporter of the right to buy, because among other things he saw it as a contribution to a more flexible labour market in terms of geographical labour mobility. It is relatively difficult for a council tenant to move around the country compared to an owner-occupier. The same concern motivated Margaret Thatcher's Government to deregulate the rental market when it developed assured private tenancies. The regulated private rented sector had contracted sharply in the 1960s and 1970s. By the 1980s, apart from so-called 'company lets', finding a private rental property had become increasingly difficult. The 1988 Housing Act significantly revived the role of the private rented sector. Between 1988 and 2008 the number of households living in privately rented accommodation doubled from just under 2 million to just under 4 million. In practice, the policies combined to represent a shift from subsidising the supply of housing – bricks and mortar – occupied initially by people in need when they took out council tenancy, to subsidising individuals in need through the Social Security system in the form of housing benefit. In 1979 spending on means tested housing benefits represented 12 per cent of public spending on housing: by 1997 it had risen to 69 per cent.

The right to buy, the channelling of capital investment in social housing through the housing associations and the reduced investment in social housing politically struck at a central plank of the post-war collectivist agenda. By the 1970s huge council estates had become synonymous with entrenched social pathology. They were perceived politically as Labour's legacy, not least because blocks of flats often had names, redolent of nostalgia for the post- war socialist Labour government, such as Clement Attlee House and Ernest Bevin Court. Although much of the council housing stock had been built by Conservative governments in the 1950s, and the much-criticised tower blocks were an initiative associated with the Conservative Housing Minister in the early 1960s, the right to buy policy was a direct political assault on Labour in its back yard. In the 1930s Herbert Morrison, the Leader of the London County Council, had famously said that Labour would build the Tories out of London. Fifty years later, Margaret Thatcher, a London Conservative MP, turned the tables. Labour opposed the policy. The local authority housing officers' union voted to disrupt the administration of the policy. With many council tenants, it was not only popular, but contributed to changing the political culture of working-class communities that since the 1940s had increasingly voted Labour. Historically, there had been a significant working-class Tory vote from the time of the great 19th century Conservative prime ministers, Benjamin Disraeli and Lord Salisbury. The Conservative Party had showed, much to the surprise of advocates of an extended franchise, that it could be competitive against the progressive parties. The Conservative Party cultivated working-class voters on non-economic questions, such as the monarchy, the union with Ireland, the Empire, defence, and national security. By the 1960s many of these matters had lost their political significance. In the 1980s having your own home and council house sales gave many previously reliable Labour voters a direct economic reason to detach themselves from Labour. The policy was hugely popular. Labour opposed it in the 1983 General Election, but by 1985 Labour accepted it. In 1981 33 per cent of the housing stock was accounted for by social housing and 56 per cent was in owner occupation. In 1991 owner occupation had risen to 67 per cent of the housing stock and social housing had fallen to 25 per cent of it. The growth in owner occupation was part of a secular rise towards owner occupation and away from rented forms of tenure. In 1961 43 per cent of the stock was accounted by owner occupation, compared to 33 per cent in the private rented sector and 25 per cent in social housing. Owner occupation rose to a peak of 67 per cent in the 1980s and it has remained there plateauing at about 68 or 69 per cent of the housing stock in the 2000s. Margaret Thatcher gave a long secular trend towards much greater owner occupation a powerful fillip through championing owning your own home, and the extension of mortgage interest relief (MIRAS) in the tax system, which she increased in the 1983 Budget, with all its distortions. She did not introduce MIRAS, nor did she introduce other changes in the tax system that favour owner occupation, such as the structure of Capital Gains Tax that exempts the main home and the abolition of taxation of imputed rent under Schedule A of the income tax system, a decision taken by Harold Macmillan's Government in the early 1960s. Owner occupation was stimulated by her sale of council houses.

In 1979 42 per cent of all individuals lived in social housing. Slightly under half of them were in the poorest two-fifths of the income distribution, but 40 per cent were in the top half of the income distribution. By 1990 the proportion of the population living in social housing had fallen to less than 25 per cent and 75 per cent of them were in lowest two-fifths of the income distribution and only 16 per cent were in the top half in terms of income. The growth in housing benefit contributed, along with the expansion of Family Credit, to the increased role of targeted or means tested benefits within the social security system. Means tested benefits rose from 15 to 30 per cent of social security budget between 1979 and 1995. This had the effect of extending the poverty trap where people in work on low incomes face very high rates of marginal benefit withdrawal as their incomes rise.

There is plenty of scope to debate the merits of Margaret

Thatcher's various policies in relation to the welfare state and NHS. Among these debates are: how well was the care in the community policy for mental health services implemented; how effective an internal market of shadow prices can be in a planned health service, free at the point of delivery; and how generous non-means tested social security transfer payments, such as child benefit and the basic National Insurance Old Age Pension should be, and the role of targeted benefits such as Family Credit. There can also be a debate about priorities within public spending.

However, the assertion that Margaret Thatcher's Government destroyed the NHS or eviscerated the welfare state cannot be reconciled with a public expenditure ratio that never fell much below 39 per cent of GDP. The lion's share of the planned spending total set out in the 1990 Autumn Statement went on social security benefits (28 per cent), health (12 per cent), and education (2 per cent), and much of the 7 per cent of the planning total going to the territorial departments was spent on health, education and social services. The big changes in government policy and functions that reduced the spending ratio were the ending of industrial subsidies, the imposition of effective external financing limits on the nationalised industries and the reduction in public spending on local authority housing. In many respects, the role of personal social services was extended through the 1989 Children Act and the National Health Service and Community Care Act.

At the same time, regardless of income, university students paid no fees. Some of the changes to social security were made in response to the changing characteristics of poverty. Historically, poverty had been associated with old age when people did not have an income from work. In the 1980s, with the growth of occupational pension funds and the growth of savings income from other sources, old age was no longer the main source of poverty. Instead poverty was increasingly associated with low income families with children. Hence, the development of Family Credit to replace and extend the old FIS in work benefit. University tuition fees were the innovation of Tony Blair's new Labour Government. Part of the new Labour critique of the Conservative Government in the 1990s was that too much money was being spent on Social Security payments and the employment trap created by the tapering of Family Credit. Whatever else she may or may not have done, Margaret Thatcher did not dismantle the welfare state.

Chapter 16: Local Government: Centralising to Liberate or Socialistic Planning?

LOCAL GOVERNMENT PRESENTED MARGARET THATCHER with a problem. It was financed by a local property tax, 'the rates', that was very unpopular. As Shadow Conservative spokesman on local government in the October 1974 General Election, she had promised to replace the domestic rating system. The Layfield Commission on local government finance that reported in 1977 still offers one of the best analyses of English local authority finance, illustrated the problem any government would have. Economic activity in the UK was and is highly unbalanced. This meant and continues to mean that the potential tax base does not match any conventional assessment of local need. To correct this, a complex nationally funded grant regime was in place. It paid for 60 per cent of council spending and the grant was distributed with the objective of facilitating a uniform level of public services throughout the country. When a group of politicians spend money that they do not have to raise in taxes that they are directly responsible for, there is a fundamental problem in terms of accountability. Many of the obvious alternatives to the rates, such as local income and sales taxes have practical difficulties and would place a potentially buoyant and elastic source of tax revenue for local councils, albeit on a lopsided economic base.

Kenneth Baker succinctly summarised the political economy of local authority taxation in the 1980s and its problem. There were 35 million electors in Britain in the mid-1980s, of whom only 18 million were liable to pay rates. Of that 18 million, 3 million paid a reduced bill and 3 million paid no bill at all. Only 12 million paid a full rates bill. In some high spending metropolitan councils, domestic ratepayers provided only 20 per cent of the rates bill. In these authorities a majority of electors could vote for higher spending on services, knowing that only a minority of electors would actually pay the bill directly.

Council elections are usually used by electors to punish governments. Councillors come and go as electorates punish the party in government nationally with little regard to local circumstances. In some parts of the country very strong local party machines (that arise out of historic strength of parties based on regional social and economic circumstances) yield permanent control of authorities to one party regardless of its performance. The effective political accountability of councils is therefore highly imperfect. Local government has historically never been trusted by central government. Their powers have been limited by statute and the law of *ultra vires*. Government funding has been accompanied by a high degree of central policy guidance and national inspection of services, such as schools, mental health services and social care. There has never been a golden age of local government. The Treasury has never trusted it and has always refused to give it effective tax-raising powers over a buoyant revenue base. Instead it has preferred to provide grants to local authorities with varying degrees of flexibility and hypothecation. The process has been consistent. National government mandates local authorities with certain statuary duties that they must carry out, such as elementary education since 1870, secondary education since 1944 and provision of residential care under the National Assistance Act 1948. The money comes from central government departments, and they try to ensure that councils spend in a manner consistent with their intentions, so there are extensive policy guidance and elaborate regimes of inspection.

The thrust of the Government's policy in the 1980s was to control local spending as part of the wider control of public spending, to protect local residents from high taxing councils and to improve the efficiency of local public services and to make services more responsive to the people using them. Rates were capped, grant was cut, legislation was passed requiring councils to expose their services to market testing and contracting, a national school curriculum was introduced and the financial control of local education authorities over schools was reduced, if not eliminated.

Most attention inevitably tends to focus on Margaret Thatcher's decision to replace the domestic rating system with the Community Charge. The unpopular 'poll tax' was levied on every adult with few exceptions. If it had been introduced on a revenue-neutral basis with no change in either spending or government grants where it raised nationally exactly the same amount as the rating system, there would have been losers. The only way they could be protected was through a generous and expensive system of transition grants. This was made more difficult because the poll tax was predicated on a naïve political conceit: that when the public saw a tax bill higher than an exemplified national average, they would punish local councillors, and through a process of rational choice force them to limit council spending and the tax. As part of this conceit, the controls on local authority spending and the capping regime that had successfully contained local spending and the rates burden were removed to give local political communities a genuine element of freedom, albeit one that could only be exercised within a highly constrained environment. This was because council spending interacted with the grant system in a manner that meant that an additional pound of spending brought about an increase in the poll tax that was greater than the spending once the council budget passed a nationally assessed notional budget. Councils, and not just Labour controlled councils, increased their spending and raised the poll tax by a proportionally greater rate through this gearing effect. Precisely because there was no central control mechanism, the Government could not hold down the bills people actually paid.

There were several other egregiously awkward features — difficulty of collection, fundamental breaches of elementary notions of equity and attempting to collect a tax from people who may not in practice have any money of their own to pay it, yet had a personal tax liability imposed on them, such as a married woman or the adult spinster who had never worked looking after parents. The Community Charge resulted in widespread political demonstrations at town halls up and down the country. There were several riots, including a major riot in Trafalgar Square in London, where the Metropolitan Police lost control of events. As well as the riots and the vitriolic politics that it provoked, the Community Charge resulted in higher local government spending and a larger proportion of local authority expenditure being financed by central government. As part of the new arrangement, business rates were taken from local councils, set nationally by central government and revenue was redistributed across councils on the basis of need. This further weakened the connection between the spending of money and the responsibility of levying the taxes to pay for it.

The average level of Community Charge necessary to yield the same revenue as the old rates was estimated in 1986 to be £189. In 1990, it turned about to be an average of £363. From 1980 to 1990 central government grant to local authorities was reduced from 60 per cent of their spending to 44 per cent. By 1991 it had increased to 70 per cent

One of the interesting features of the episode was that many people who were most angered by the poll tax were people who were not necessarily offended by the structure of the tax. They were attracted to the notion that everyone should pay something. What offended them was the debate about local council funding that made them aware of the scale of local government spending and they doubted the value and efficiency of this spending.

The record of the Thatcher Government in relation to local government is in many respects a much more fundamental one than the political disaster of the poll tax. It amounted to an energetic attempt to centralise it to make it better, to make it more responsive to local communities, to overcome its inertia and to make it more efficient. The principal efficiency measures were the creation of the Audit Commission and the requirement to market test local government services. The Audit Commission looked across the system and identified best practice and offered policy guidance that exemplified it. This approach drew on the paradigm offered by operations analysis. Many of the Audit Commission's senior executives had in previous careers worked on operations analysis for nationalised industries, such as the National Coal Board. Such an approach exhibits the limitations that are at the heart of the failure of socialist planned economies. The true paradox of Margaret Thatcher's approach to local government and indeed to the wider public sector was that what she would recognise as a recipe for failure in the economy as a whole, she applied to local government and the public sector. The paradox is not that she centralised to liberate, but that she turned to policy approaches that in practice were at the heart of indicative planning that she would normally have rejected as being essentially socialist and unworkable in the long run. They did yield some significant shorter term improvements in efficiency, but could not generate sustained or dynamic improvements in performance.

The broad direction of these policies was maintained by the Conservative and Labour governments that followed. New Labour took things a stage further, both with extensive targets and much greater use of hypothecated grants, as well as a baroque inspection regime that rated councils. The result was that a large increase in spending failed to deliver improved outcomes. Instead, measured productivity fell in public services provided by local authorities in the 10 years to 2007. Likewise, the Conservative-Liberal Democrat Coalition Government, despite acknowledging the importance of local discretion, has done little to give councils significantly greater autonomy. Although the Coalition has removed many of the New Labour targets and cut the plethora of hypothecated grants, it has taken further steps to nationalise school policy, and frozen the council tax to defuse the issue of its cost.

It is better therefore to place Margaret Thatcher in the mainstream of British politics when it comes to local government, rather than thinking of her as unusual, because of the poll tax. The truth is that her governments and ministers, such as Michael Heseltine, the Secretary of State responsible for establishing the Audit Commission, did not make a better fist of a difficult position than any other government, such as those of Ted Heath or Tony Blair and Gordon Brown. Despite all the effort put into establishing the Audit Commission, reorganising the metropolitan counties, abolishing the Greater London Council and the Inner London Education Authority, changing the local authority tax base, it did not make much difference in terms of its fundamental defects and the practical difficulties of combining efficient public services with effective local accountability.

Strangely enough, the obvious things that a Conservative government could have done that would have made a difference were not done. Ending national collective pay bargaining both for councils and the rest of the public sector would have been a major contributor to cost control and greater efficiency. It would have made local labour markets more flexible, especially if it had been accompanied by regional rates for Social Security transfer payments for people of working age and if such benefits were set taking into account local labour markets' conditions.

The atmosphere in local government at that time has also to be recognised. The Prime Minister did not seek a confrontation with local government. It was presented to her on a plate. Her view of local government was indubitably coloured, as she had been

Secretary of State for Education and Science in the early 1970s. She had doubts about its efficiency and competence. She was concerned to control overall local authority spending as part of wider public spending. Yet even if she had not harboured such instincts, she faced local authorities that were determined to confront her Government. Liverpool, Sheffield, Derbyshire, Lambeth and the GLC in London were led by leaders such as David Bookbinder, Ted Knight and Ken Livingstone. These authorities were controlled by radical hard left leaderships whose principal raison d'être was confronting Tories in general, and Tory ministers in particular.

There is a dimension of Margaret Thatcher's long period in office relating to local government that is often overlooked. Several of the principal pieces of legislation that shape the day-to-day functioning of local authorities were her measures. Among them are the 1988 Education Act, the Children Act 1989 and the National Health and Community Care Act 1990. The Children Act and the Community Care Act are landmarks in social services reform, that as Lord Laming argues, have stood the test of time. They were not in any way incidental or passed by accident. They were measures the Prime Minister was fully involved with and interested in. As Lord Laming, a former President of the National Association of Directors of Social Services perceives it, Margaret Thatcher supported them, because she believed they would yield practical benefits that would help people and families in difficult circumstances. She saw the need for the state 'to protect children in real danger from malign parents', as she put it in her memoirs.

The abolition of the GLC contributed to the visceral loathing of the Prime Minister. The musical *The Ratepayers' Iolanthe* in 1984 was one of the great satirical events of the second half of the 20th century. As a piece of polemical political comedy there is some superb competition, not least from *Spitting Image*. It is these and the bitterness of the coal strike, along with folk memories of the poll tax that maintain the lurid caricature of Margaret Thatcher that is so present in contemporary popular culture. Most of what is attributed to her personally, to the actions of her governments or to her ideas, is by this reflex, fanciful as well as toxic.

Margaret Thatcher: The economics of creative destruction

Chapter 17: Downfall

IN MANY RESPECTS, Margaret Thatcher's opposition to the ERM and her attitude to European integration was her nemesis. The ERM was central to her disagreement with Nigel Lawson, and it was his resignation as Chancellor that ended Thatcherism as an effective political force with a realistic hold on power. It was the stuff of Greek tragedy. Nigel Lawson was a very powerful minister who saw that her writ ran throughout Whitehall on spending, taxing, borrowing, how the labour market worked, the role of wages in the economy, the contribution of regional policy and the reform of the supply performance of the economy. The Chancellor gave the Prime Minister intellectual muscle and he buttressed it with a robust political authority, both inside the Government and beyond.

The Prime Minister's clarity in expressing her opposition to the single currency solidified political hostility to her both within the Government and among her parliamentary party. It was her attitude to European integration that galvanised her most senior colleagues, who were in a position to set about destroying her hold on office. The unpopularity of the Community Charge probably had more influence on her backbench MPs. But the issue that really made her vulnerable more than anything else was what would now be called the omnishambles of monetary policy.

In 1990, inflation was 10 per cent and interest rates were 15 per cent. The Conservative achievement had been to get inflation down. Now it was back in double digits and interest rates were at a nightmare level for many homeowners who had brought their homes with mortgages on the promise of Thatcherite prosperity. The opinion polls pointed to a Labour victory and a realistic reading of the economy pointed to a long and hard recession to get inflation down. What was more, the ERM framework probably precluded any fancy footwork by the Chancellor to stimulate the economy closer to the election.

There was also a sense of envy and revulsion among some Conservative MPs about the Prime Minister's style. By 1990 it was not best described as presidential or regal, but rather as imperial. It was the clothes, the international statesperson in the superleague, not so much on the world stage, but above it. She rarely appeared in Parliament apart from questions, statements and voting divisions. When she did, the Prime Minister swept in with an entourage of private secretaries, officials from Number 10 and the Cabinet Office and a Special Branch close protection security detail. This was a legacy of the October 1984 bombing of the Grand Hotel in Brighton by the Provisional IRA, and the police advice that the Prime Minister was at greatest threat of assassination when she was in the Palace of Westminster. However, it compounded the impression of a Prime Minister with 12 police motorcycle outriders too many. Her last speech at the Lord Mayor's Banquet in the Guildhall in 1990 was the final straw for these MPs. She was wearing a magnificent dress with a long cloak and a very high collar. It was truly, extraordinarily, spectacular. A sort of Elizabeth I meets Catherine the Great rig-out with assistance from Marilyn Monroe's hairdresser. It was certainly a choice of dress that damaged the Prime Minister politically. There was also a range of other motivations: the spite of the reshuffled ministers and a feeling of resentment among right wing MPs who were strong supporters of the Prime Minister. A number of these considered that they had been overlooked for ministerial promotion, when other people, who though obviously able, were promoted, despite the fact that they did not support or share the Prime Minister's vision in the way that they did.

The Prime Minister's manner in handling ministerial colleagues also contributed to her downfall. Margaret Thatcher had genuine friends among Labour MPs, including several left-wing MPs. These friends included Fenner Brockway, Maurice Edelman, Eric Heffer and Harold Lever. She showed great consideration and courtesy to Opposition Members of Parliament. She was also very kind to civil servants and other people who worked for her directly at 10 Downing Street, and they were often fond of her personally. Yet the same kindness and courtesy was not extended to her ministerial colleagues. If anything, it was quite the reverse.

It was generally known that Margaret Thatcher had been rude to Sir Geoffrey Howe shortly before his resignation. His resignation statement in the House of Commons was a masterpiece of devastating political damage. It contributed to persuading Michael Heseltine to challenge Margaret Thatcher in the leadership election in November 1990. People who were political friends of the Prime Minister and who served her loyally, often were left with sad personal memories of Margaret Thatcher being rude to them. A good example is Baroness Young, a long-serving minister of state who was briefly in her Cabinet (indeed, the only woman to serve in a Thatcher Cabinet). Janet Young knew Margaret Thatcher for many years and remained politically loyal to her. She was a cultivated woman, a former Leader of Oxford City Council, married to a don, the Vice Principal of Jesus College. She confided to a friend that on one occasion that Margaret Thatcher had been very rude to her, and in fact had spoken to her in a manner that even her husband, Geoffrey, would never have dared to do. This sort of behaviour in a politician is never prudent. Over the years it was a factor that aggravated hostility to her within the highest reaches of her administration. The way she handled her relationships with ministerial colleagues was a contributing factor to the resentments that led to her downfall.

When the end finally came, it presented a practical difficulty to Treasury. Margaret Thatcher as Prime Minister was technically the First Lord of the Treasury. This meant that the Treasury was in charge of looking after the seals of office that she had to surrender. As luck would have it, so many years had passed since Margaret Thatcher had been appointed that the Treasury establishment department — the personnel department in any other organisation — had mislaid them.

Chapter 18: Margaret Thatcher's Public Personality and Symbiotic Relationship with her Opponents

FROM THE START THERE WAS AN ELECTRIFYING QUALITY about Margaret Thatcher. In some ways this is apposite, because Michael Faraday, the pioneer demonstrator of the properties of electricity, was her favourite scientist. This quality was on repeated display throughout her life and career. Whether it was the speech at Kensington Town Hall that earned her the sobriquet of "Iron Lady" from the Soviet press, her address to the General Assembly of the Church of Scotland, or the interview she gave to *Liberation* in July 1989 about the French Revolution, she had the capacity to make arresting comments that offered a sort of high powered commonsense that infuriated her political opponents. Like lightning rods struck in an electric storm, her opponents tended to respond with an intemperate rage that was often mistaken on fact and argument. These intense controversies provoked by Margaret Thatcher expressing her thoughts moved the political debate in a direction that often turned out to be anathema to her antagonists. Their intemperate responses carried little traction with the ordinary voter and facilitated the radical movement of opinion in her direction. Margaret Thatcher was fortunate in her enemies and her opponents. It was not simply that Michael Foot was implausible as a Prime Minster in any circumstances, and certainly even less plausible in his eighth decade, or that Arthur Scargill was wholly unreasonable and foolishly reckless, but many of her opponents in their revulsion at her ideas helped to create the fissures that would crack the cement of previously settled arguments. The left-wing leadership of many Labour local authorities enabled the Labour Opposition to be parodied as the "loony left in the town hall", a dire warning of what Labour would be like in government.

Mr Foot was in many respects an admirable person, who personally got on very well with Margaret Thatcher. But as Leader of the Labour Party in the early 1980s he gave the impression, as Queen Victoria had unfairly said of William Gladstone, that he was 'old, mad and dangerous'. Neil Kinnock, who led the Labour Party from 1983 for the remainder of Margaret Thatcher's period in 10 Downing Street, was an energetic and in many ways effective Leader of the Labour Party. Mr Kinnock faced down the hard left of his party, excised the Militant Tendency, a sort of Trotskyite party within the Labour party, and began to move Labour policy away from the Alternative Economic Strategy. Although Margaret Thatcher won the 1987 general election handsomely, under Neil Kinnock's leadership Labour fought a most effective campaign. It was probably more effective in its execution than that of the Conservatives. Mr Kinnock never, however, acquired the political authority that Margaret Thatcher exuded even when she was in Opposition, a period when she most certainly did not have it all her own way, with formidable opponents such as Mr Wilson and Mr Callaghan.

Mr Kinnock was a very good conference platform speaker and an effective television communicator, but had great difficulty in commanding the attention and respect of the House of Commons. Most Leaders of the Opposition, including Margaret Thatcher in her time, have that difficulty. Yet Mr Kinnock found it particularly difficult to rise to the occasion when it was needed in Parliament.

Margaret Thatcher: The economics of creative destruction

During the Westland crisis in 1986, one of the worst domestic political crises Margaret Thatcher faced, Mr Kinnock failed to drive home important legal, constitutional and political points in a debate where the Prime Minister was vulnerable. This was in marked contrast to the performance of the Shadow Trade and Industry Secretary John Smith, who deployed all the forensic skills of a QC to great effect in the debates about the funding and ownership of a company that made military helicopters.

When Michael Heseltine, the Secretary for Defence, who had resigned over the Westland affair, finally challenged Margaret Thatcher for the Leadership of the Conservative Party in 1990, Mr Kinnock made a significant mistake. Instead of allowing the divided Conservatives to stew in their own bitter internal battle, Mr Kinnock chose to table a motion of no confidence in Her Majesty's Government. This galvanised the Conservative Party to unite and gave Margaret Thatcher an extraordinary parliamentary platform to lay out not just a defence of her 11 years in power, but a manifesto of her vision for Britain's future. In effect, Mr Kinnock facilitated Margaret Thatcher's greatest parliamentary performance.

Leonid Brezhnev and the geriatric Soviet leadership in the 1970s and early 1980s were a political gift for any Conservative politician campaigning against socialism. Thatcher derided them for building a system that needed a wall to keep their people in. They gave her a backhanded compliment of calling her the "Iron Lady", which turned out to be very helpful to the first woman to lead a political party, when she felt she needed to show her mettle.

So there was genuine serendipity in the opposition and enemies that she faced. But that should not belie recognition of the fact that she also created her own luck by audaciously challenging the established consensus. It should also be noted that she led the Conservatives in Opposition against two of the most effective politicians of their day, Mr Wilson and Mr Callaghan, and won power by defeating a Labour Party led by Mr Callaghan, even if he was handicapped by the presence of Mr Foot and Mr Benn.

Chapter 19: A Scientist in Government

MARGARET THATCHER, AS WELL AS BEING the country's first woman Prime Minister, was the first modern Prime Minister who was a trained scientist. She read chemistry at Oxford and then worked as a research chemist in industry. This dimension of Margaret Thatcher's experience, made her different from other senior ministers. She was plainly an intelligent and clever person in the normal, grammatical meaning of those words. She was not considered an outstanding student in the Chemistry Department at Oxford in the 1940s, but she was certainly considered a well-organised and competent chemist by her tutor, who said she could be relied on to approach science questions in a thoroughly capable way. Her training as a scientist coloured her approach to policy, which placed great emphasis on the accumulation of facts and arguments and then subjecting them to rigorous analysis. This was very much part of her determination to be well briefed. It was not necessarily the exhibition of an intellectually brilliant mind, but it was most certainly the working method of a hugely capable person, who brought great application to all that she did.

There is a distasteful pastime that amuses the British establishment that attempts to rank the intellectual capabilities of people who are clearly very intelligent and to find ways of suggesting that their minds are somehow imperfect. A famous example of it is Sir Isaiah Berlin's comment about another Fellow of All Souls College Oxford, the immensely clever diplomat Lord Sherfield , that he had 'one of the finest second-class minds in Britain'. A good example of this silliness was when Roy Jenkins chose to describe Tony Blair as possessing a second-class mind. Margaret Thatcher may have appeared to have a less refined mind than that of some of her Cabinet colleagues, but any suggestion that she was not intellectually as good as them fails to take account of the asymmetry between her education and theirs. Most of the time she was dealing with matters, such as economics and foreign affairs, which were often their special subjects, but they were not within her original university education. This meant that she sometimes expressed herself clumsily and explored unusual propositions. The asymmetry between their relative ignorance of all science and technology and her disadvantage in terms of history and political economy was very much in her favour.

She retained a serious and broad interest in science and technology and was not afraid of getting to grips with policy briefings on those matters. Many ministers and senior civil servants take little serious interest in these, apart from the bare minimum they have to do to get through the meeting. Lord May, the former Chief Scientific Adviser and former President of the Royal Society, has pointed out that it was Margaret Thatcher who re-established the role of the Chief Scientific Adviser and set up the the Advisory Council on Science and Technology, and frequently chaired it, which no subsequent Prime Minister has done. The scientists who worked directly with her as Prime Minister provide ample testimony to the fact that the scientific method was embedded in her approach to policy development and to her interest in the subject area. In this way she was genuinely different from other ministers. It was also evident to industrialists who met the Prime Minister when she visited their factories and research laboratories.

To say that Margaret Thatcher remains a hugely controversial figure among scientists is to fail to convey the continuing sense of outrage that they feel towards her. In the 1980s there were significant reductions in university funding and spending on research in government departments and government funding of research in industry. Moreover, government funding for research was centralised and the proportion of it channelled through the national research funding councils was increased. There was also a change in focus, with greater emphasis being placed on funding research that supported economic growth. The initial cuts in research spending in the early 1980s permanently embittered much of the science community.

Part of this change of focus emphasised the need for universities and publicly funded research bodies to collaborate with business and industry. This is sometimes perceived as being part of the ending of a national industrial strategy that from the 1950s amounted to a government-led and funded technological and science policy directed at achieving national political and military objectives. Here the complaint is that there was no attempt to support national champions. As David Edgerton commented in 'Privatiser and Nationaliser' in *Research Fortnight* in April 2013, this was the dismantling of a distinctive British approach to industrial R&D and technology, and meant that in future there would be no more Concordes or British-designed gas-cooled nuclear reactors. He argues that this was an inconsistency. Government spending on the sciences was supposed to contribute to economic growth, yet the necessary industrial strategy to translate the research into marketable products was abandoned.

This perception of what was done and why is interestingly at odds with what Margaret Thatcher thought she was doing. In her memoirs she wrote that, in her view, too much government funding of science was going to military research and to industry. She therefore tried to ensure that government spending was concentrated on fundamental research. She set up a sub-committee of the Economic Committee of the Cabinet (EST), chaired by herself, to ensure that a new approach was taken to funding science. It went through departmental science budgets, breaking them down between basic science and support for innovation. Greater emphasis was given to basic research and less was placed on supporting innovation by sector. In her memoirs she explains that she thought pure science and the universities had lost out, with too much government money going into the development of products for the market that could be left to industry itself to fund. She comments that 'the greatest economic benefits of scientific research have always resulted from advances in knowledge rather than search for specific applications.' Although a highly instrumental approach to science is attributed to Margaret Thatcher, it is probably a misattribution.

After the initial cut to university budgets, science funding to the universities from the funding councils rose significantly. As David Edgerton puts it, while the scientific elite pleaded poverty, the university labs were overflowing. While the proportion of world research coming from the UK may have been diminishing, the absolute research output went up. I am not going to adjudicate on the merits of channelling funding through the research councils or the merits of greater centralisation of science spending within Whitehall, but I am not persuaded that dismantling the techno-industrial strategy was a mistake. It is reassuring to know that there will be no more Concordes. The few we had were far too expensive.

The overall legacy, while it may have been contentious, did not eviscerate British science. The relative quantity of papers produced may have fallen, but the absolute number published rose. The quality, moreover, held up well; as an American scientist, John T Finn writing in *Science* in August 2001 noted, in the mid 1980s to mid 1990s the UK produced more papers per capita than many countries and there were more citations per paper. British researchers received more citations per pound spent on research than papers from nearly all other countries, including the US.

There is one thing that most scientists recognise, which is that it was Margaret Thatcher's training as a scientist that stimulated her interest in atmospheric temperature change. She followed the work of the British Antarctic Survey, grasped the implications of the hole in the ozone layer that was identified by the Survey in the 1980s and recognised the implications that climate change could have. This led to her making her speech to the Royal Society that put the issue of climate change on the international policy agenda. She found vivid ways of conveying her message, telling the Conservative Party conference in 1988, that 'no generation has a freehold on this earth. All we have is a life tenancy with a full repairing lease. This Government intends to meet the terms of that lease in full'.

Chapter 20: The Limits of the Thatcher Agenda

MARGARET THATCHER SUPPORTED PRIVATE ENTERPRISE and recognised the importance of business success and the need to reward it. She also recognised that the public sector was chronically inefficient and needed to become more productive. As a result, she married her support for free enterprise and business to the objective of making the public sector more efficient by introducing private sector management techniques and contracting out to the private sector. There was nothing wrong with this in principle, and it was in many respects sensible. Yet it resulted in mistaking the work of delivering public services for a kind of faux business management, where the public receiving the service or being regulated were regarded as customers. The truth is that a public sector organisation operating without a hard budget constraint is not a business subject to the same disciplines as a private business operating in a contested market. There are many merits in contracting out, but it merely shifts the point at which inefficiency is exhibited. Even with competitive tendering, there is a great deal of opportunity for rent-seeking at the expense of the taxpayer.

Applying a business management culture to Whitehall and its executive agencies became a substitute for genuine and effective public sector reform. The enterprise culture in government went too far. The Government was too cautious about public service reform and limiting the role of trade unions in public sector employee management. By the time Margaret Thatcher left office, effective trade union power was something confined to the public sector. In the years that followed, on the basis of all the normal tests – trade union density, proportion of employees covered by collective agreements and identifiable trade union wages levels, effective trade union power only continued to flourish in local government and the national public service. Little or no progress was made in dismantling national collective pay bargaining in the public sector. This contributed to public services that continued to be inefficient and increasingly contributed to local and regional labour markets where wages were above market clearing levels. These local labour markets increasingly became uncompetitive and detached from internationally contested markets. The combination of public sector pay premiums arising out of national public sector terms and conditions and national rates of Social Security transfer payments that did not take account of local circumstances, created the conditions where deindustrialisation became a wider and entrenched demarketisation. A similar process occurred in East Germany after unification in 1990, where non-clearing nationally agreed wages and benefits locked the East German Länder into permanent structural unemployment.

By 1989, 10 years after Margaret Thatcher's election victory in May 1979, the Thatcher project had run out of steam. There simply was not the political appetite to carry out obviously necessary further reform consistent with the agenda that had been pursued by Margaret Thatcher in opposition and government. There was a reluctance to take measures that would enable the ratio of general government expenditure to be stabilised at around 35 per cent of GDP over the economic cycle rather than a figure that was closer to 40 or 41 per cent. In part this reflected the personal political commitments that the Prime Minister had inevitably accumulated. Before the 1983 election she had made it clear that the National

Health Service free at the point of use was 'safe in our hands'. Her commitment to the Nottingham miners as a result of their continuing to work and helping to break the coal strike, for example, meant that the National Coal Board could not be properly sorted out. Yet it was more than this. It was a lack of serious appetite on the part of the Government to look again at difficult matters that had already been the subject of contentious change. A good example of this was Social Security. This had been the subject of the Fowler Social Security reforms. There was little appetite to reopen them in order to bring about localised benefit rates or to limit or means test child benefit.

Norman Lamont, the Chief Secretary of the Treasury, who went on to be John Major's campaign manager in the Conservative leadership election in 1990 and then served as his first Chancellor of the Exchequer, thought that Thatcherism was dead some time before the Prime Minister left office. Margaret Thatcher's Government had in effect used up its political space. It was elected to restore financial discipline, control trade union power and to create a modern market economy that could properly function. By 1989 it had not only accomplished that political mandate, but it had started to travel beyond it. In 1989 Nigel Lawson and his ministers and special advisers put a lot of work into trying to marshal a major speech on the next 10 years. Despite various drafts being put together, it was not possible to construct a politically cogent agenda, because each worthwhile idea was perceived as too difficult or already pre-empted by previous political commitments.

During John Major's first administration it was almost as if Margaret Thatcher governed Britain from her political grave, in the same way that Oliver Cromwell governed Britain from his actual grave in the year after his death in 1658. John Major embarked on some distinctive novel policies such as the Citizens' Charter and took the first steps towards the Private Finance Initative in the Autumn Statement of 1992. Little was done to carry the Thatcherite agenda forward. Instead, a series of measures consistent with it were

The Limits of the Thatcher Agenda

taken, such as removing coal subsidies, the privatisation of British Rail and Peter Lilley's reforms to Social Security, including the equalisation of the pension age for men and women at 65.

The New Labour project adjusted to the practical policy consensus forged by Margaret Thatcher's governments. There was no return to nationalisation. The fundamentals of the reform of trade union law were left in place: unions still needed properly conducted ballots before they could enjoy immunity from tort. The Bank of England was made operationally independent and the inflation target introduced after the ERM debacle was slightly relaxed, but retained. While the tax burden was increased by widening the tax base, the basic rate of income tax and the top marginal rate of tax remained at much lower levels than those set by Sir Geoffrey Howe in the early 1980s. Tony Blair and Gordon Brown did not forge a new policy consensus; instead they worked within the consensus that Margaret Thatcher had established.

The political success of the New Labour project illustrated a significant dimension of democratic politics. This is that the political party that forges a particular policy consensus is not always perceived by the electorate as the best party to manage and work within it. The Attlee Labour Government in 1945 established the post-war Keynesian welfare consensus and the mixed partly nationalised economy. Yet in the 1950s it was the Conservative Party that was perceived as the natural party of government. They may have been in office, but the post-war governments of Churchill, Eden and Macmillan stuck carefully to the script of Butskellism. That does not mean that while operating within the constraints of a prevailing consensus, a party in government cannot make progress in tailoring its policies to achieve its political objectives. New Labour effectively demonstrated this with its massive discretionary increase in public expenditure and the way the tax and benefit system was modified to concentrate greater discretionary assistance to households with children in the bottom third of income distribution.

Likewise, the political party that creates a new policy consensus is in some ways handicapped by it. Even when it is out of office, the policies are still their policies. Nationalisation was a millstone around Labour's neck, until Margaret Thatcher relieved Labour of that burden. Much of the controversy generated in creating a new policy consensus also sticks to the party that forges it in a way that can be unhelpful in future electoral contests. The Conservative Party has plainly been handicapped by the controversies that Margaret Thatcher created as she reformed and transformed modern Britain.

The Limits of the Thatcher Agenda

Chapter 21: Thatcherism as an Ideology

THE TERM "THATCHERISM" WAS COINED BY NIGEL LAWSON, her long-serving Chancellor of the Exchequer who, with Sir Geoffrey Howe, worked closely with her in opposition and played a central part in constructing the Conservative economic agenda. Nigel Lawson saw Thatcherism as a revival of interest in long-standing ideas that had influenced the Conservative Party from the time of Sir Robert Peel in the 1830s to the Conservative Party led by Winston Churchill in the 1950s. These ideas could be found in the writings of Edmund Burke, Adam Smith, and David Hume. Thatcherism was a reaction against the post-war Keynesian consensus that the Conservative Party had embraced between 1951 and 1975. It in many respects represented a return to a previous liberal economic consensus of which the Conservative Party had been part in the 19th and early 20th century. It drew heavily on the ideas and work of Milton Freidman and Frederic Hayek, because most of the immediate challenges were economic and directly related to inflation and the difficulty of maintaining price stability. It was liberal and empirical in outlook, couched in a series of propositions that expressed reservations about a large public sector and an overreaching state. Among them were ambitions to contain public spending, to reduce marginal tax rates and to lower government borrowing. These were presented as ideological propositions, because the Conservative Party had to confront a highly ideologically motivated Labour Party in the 1970s, even though by that time the social democratic consensus on Keynesian economic management was in intellectual disarray.

Greater use of the price mechanism, free markets and financial discipline were easily married with traditional Conservative concerns about traditional institutions, strong defence and a commitment to law and order. These were things that had occupied Conservative governments from the time of Lord Salisbury in 1886. The commitment to patriotism and a strong state supported by well equipped armed services was amplified by the tensions of the Cold War. The reflex of supporting traditional institutions was strengthened by the debate about devolution in the 1970s. The liberal economic rhetoric that was used to make the case for economic reform gave a useful coherence and cover to a wider range of traditional ideas that were part of a Tory agenda.

Margaret Thatcher had a High Tory approach to the constitution. Under her leadership, the Conservative Party rejected devolution and wrapped itself in a passionate defence of the Union straight out of the pages of A. V. Dicey's *Law of the Constitution*. This reading of the British constitution placed great emphasis on the unlimited sovereignty of the Imperial Parliament at Westminster. She was suspicious of any change to the procedures of the legislature and probably regretted the one major institutional reform that the Conservatives carried out when they were first elected in 1979; the introduction of the select committee system. In the 1970s, there was increasing concern about the power the executive exercised with little, if any, effective check from Parliament. This arose from the fact that the same political machine that gave the executive office normally gave it control over Parliament. This concern was powerfully expressed by Lord Hailsham, the Conservative former Lord Chancellor, in his Richard Dimbleby BBC Lecture in 1976 when he called it an "elective dictatorship". In Opposition, the

Conservative Party advocated the establishment of departmental select committees to scrutinise the conduct of ministers. In government the pledge was fulfilled, to the continuing irritation of Conservative ministers. Margaret Thatcher opposed, or more usually blocked, all other constitutional reform proposals, whether it was reform of the House of Lords, televising the House of Commons, or introducing a bill of rights. It is a misreading of her to regard her as a liberal in the classical liberal sense or in any systematic way.

Margaret Thatcher's commitment to personal freedom, property rights, balanced budgets and free markets should not confuse anyone into imagining that she was a classical liberal or the reincarnation of William Gladstone in a skirt. Fundamental freedoms could be pragmatically modified and curtailed. The curb on broadcasting by members of the IRA offers a good example of this pragmatism in relation to freedom of speech. State and military power could and was ruthlessly deployed. Margaret Thatcher believed in strong defences, fulfilled the UK NATO commitment to raise defence spending to 3 per cent of GDP, and showed in the Falklands conflict a willingness to take great military risks to secure political and national interests. Likewise, there was nothing systematic in her support for free markets and property rights. Margaret Thatcher was quite comfortable employing systematic market distortions in order to achieve her social and political objectives, and the interests of 'our people'. This is best exemplified by her attachment to mortgage interest relief to promote home ownership. It was also evident in her approach to the nationalised industries. The Post Office for her was always going to be the Royal Mail, and after the miners' strike she was determined to maintain coal subsidies to support miners in the Midlands who had worked during the strike and had contributed to breaking it, even when their pits were uneconomic.

Margaret Thatcher was probably uncomfortable with the notion that she was trying to create an ideology and may have regarded any such suggestion, initially, as a sort of calculated political insult.

Thatcherism as an Ideology

Her opponents on the Marxist left, however, saw her as a formidable ideological enemy and went on to construct a paradigm that was intended to describe Thatcherism as an ideology. This Marxist critique simplified and distilled a series of ideas and policy measures that were muddled, inconsistent and contingent, into a series of propositions that appeared both coherent and novel. Her critics gave a superficial, but powerful coherence to her thoughts and actions that was greater than they deserved. In many respects, her Marxist critics unintentionally constructed an account of Margaret Thatcher's thought and record in government that gives them a continuing relevance and applicability that they would not have achieved without the stylised Gramscian critique that they received from the contributors to *Marxism Today*. Margaret Thatcher's political admirers and disciples left to their own devices could never have constructed as compelling an ideological statement. In many respects, this is the greatest service that her opponents offered her.

Defining Thatcherism as a coherent ideology, albeit one exhibiting tensions and inconsistencies, the contributors to *Marxism Today* provided a set of ideas and an agenda that could be applied in other times and in other places. Much of Margaret Thatcher's true legacy is time-specific. It arises from particular circumstances and opportunities that are unlikely to be repeated again, such as the Falklands war and the miners' strike. Yet the agenda of liberal markets and a strong state, deregulation, privatisation, extending the role of the markets and limiting the role of the state has an applicability that is not tied to Britain or to Britain in the 1980s. For centre-right and right-wing politicians the world over, it offers a starting place and set of propositions to work back from.

Conservatives, as opposed to Liberals, did not have a rough and ready set of propositions to turn to before Thatcher and Reagan. Much of both their agendas and their legacies are drawn from a wider liberal tradition exemplified by Gladstone's dislike of 'construction' and income tax. But it was not in any way confined by

Gladstonian fastidiousness about retrenchment of public expenditure in all areas and caution in defence and foreign affairs.

Thatcher was not an intellectual. She was plainly very clever and she was interested in ideas and in the ideas of intellectuals that appeared to offer convenient support and suggestions that would help her on her chosen path, hence her interest in the thought of Hayek and Milton Friedman. She was careful not to sign up to academic or intellectual paradigms, even when she was attracted to them or probably shared them. She was very careful to say, for example, that the natural rate of unemployment was an 'academic' concept and not a statement of the Government's labour market policy. She picked up ideas to help her make a case for common sense propositions, as she saw them. This was particularly the case during the period when she led the Opposition. With Sir Keith Joseph she tried to work up an alternative 'philosophy' to socialism. This required a highly stylised account of socialism in order to construct its free market antithesis. It was practical and empirical. The practical imperative was to have an account that described what was going on and did not end up with the conclusion that what was needed was an incomes policy, because the unions would not work with a Tory government. She needed an alternative economic case to argue against the Keynesian economics mediated through Labour's social democratic agenda largely constructed by Anthony Crosland in his books, *The Future of Socialism* and *The Conservative Enemy*. The empirical dimension came from the fact that much of the critique of the neo-Keynesian policy consensus was based on empirical rather than theoretical criticism. This is best illustrated by Milton Friedman's approach to monetarism. It also fitted into Margaret Thatcher's own interest in facts and measurement, as well as the older Tory tradition of sceptical empiricism.

It was an adventurous path. Tories traditionally were cautious of change. By 1975 Margaret Thatcher's world had changed out of all recognition from her childhood and she did not like it. The changes appeared to have wrought chaos and disaster. This meant that she was prepared to demolish the post-war consensus. The sobriquet "radical" was often applied to her. Yet it was not just radicalism that she exhibited, but iconoclasm.

In 1979 the Conservative Party offered an economic agenda that promised to roll back the state, reduce public spending as a share of national income and limit the scope of collectivist institutions. It explicitly rejected the post-war Keynesian welfare consensus. Problems that had been evaded for decades were to be addressed. The Conservative programme marked a radical break with what had gone before. It was the Marxian economists who recognised that it was 'by no means stupid or ill considered, it had a fairly coherent idea with what was wrong with British capitalism and how it can be put right'. Robert Rowthorn recognised it as the product of intense effort by right-wing thinkers and a 'determined attempt to come to grips with a problem which governments have evaded for decades'. The Marxian analysis recognised that the British economy needed modernisation and competition and that market forces would bring that modernisation about by breaking up the existing market structure. In effect, a process of Schumpetarian creative destruction that had been evaded for years would be allowed to take place.

Margaret Thatcher: The economics of creative destruction

Chapter 22: The Economic Legacy of Margaret Thatcher

THE CENTRAL PROPOSITIONS OF THE CONSERVATIVE PLATFORM in 1979 were to control inflation, restore financial stability and to create the conditions where a market economy could flourish and living standards could rise in the manner that they did in other advanced economies. The ambition was to halt relative national economic decline.

Inflation was brought down to manageable levels of around 3 to 4 per cent in the first half of the 1980s. This was a great achievement. It was accompanied by inevitable transition costs. These costs were aggravated by two things. The first was more than 20 years of state-sponsored policies that had attempted to avoid necessary and uncomfortable change. The second was an inflexible labour market that meant that adjustment to a malign shock took the form of a quantity rather than a price adjustment. Real wages continued to grow while unemployment rose, and unemployment continued to rise even when the economy had been expanding for several years. Inflation fell in the UK as part of a wider international process of disinflation that lowered commodity prices. Weaker international commodity prices played an important part in contributing to lower UK inflation. This international disinflation reflected the discretionary monetary policy actions of other countries, notably

Mr Paul Volcker's brand of monetarism in the US, based on reserve targeting from October 1979 to August 1982. At its best, the UK's improved performance in terms of inflation was in line with international progress, rather than outperforming other advanced economies.

There were serious errors in monetary policy in the mid-1980s that returned inflation to double digits, peaking at over 10 per cent in 1990. Vigorous policy action was then taken to bring inflation back under control that resulted in further heavy transition costs to return inflation to an acceptable level. This resulted in a recession in the early 1990s that was longer in duration, albeit more shallow in terms of the loss of output, than that in the early 1980s. This second protracted loss of output can be fairly attributed to Margaret Thatcher's Government. The origins of the inflation were located in the Lawson boom, and the extent and duration of the loss of output necessary to correct it were aggravated by the decision to place sterling within the ERM. The character of the recession in the early 1990s was very different from that in the early 1980s. Whereas the deep fall in output in the 1980s was concentrated in the North and the West Midlands, and in manufacturing as obsolete industrial capacity was eliminated, in the 1990s the impact of the recession was felt much more severely in the south of England. This was because of the negative equity that arose from the fall in house prices.

The institutional arrangements for the conduct of monetary policy were not resolved. The Bank of England that had been nationalised in 1945 remained in a master-servant relationship, with HM Treasury as the master. The important and complex issues relating to public sector debt management, banking supervision and interest rate setting were all unresolved. There were clear conflicts of interests, as well as repeated policy errors principally on the part of the Bank of England in relation to the more technical part of its responsibilities. The record of the Bank of England in terms of banking supervision in the 1980s was poor, as the BCCI episode illustrated. Too often, decisions on interest rates were complicated by the central bank's role in issuing debt and not wanting to make it difficult to sell its bonds. The central bank's operations in the money market through the discount houses to manage day-to-day liquidity were ineffective, leading to erratic and volatile overnight interest rates. Nigel Lawson had proposed an institutional framework to the Prime Minister that would have set up an independent central bank. In fairness to Margaret Thatcher, there was a problem with making the Bank of England independent. There is in general a good case for independent central banks in democratic societies. Yet there remained a question about whether this particular central bank should be made independent.

While inflation was brought down in the UK in the early 1980s and again in the early 1990s, the UK retained a greater propensity to generate inflation than other advanced economies. Even when inflation is low, the UK appears to need a tighter domestic monetary policy than other economies in terms of interest rates. Despite having flexible and efficient product and labour markets, the UK exhibits higher inflation than other advanced economies. Part of the explanation probably relates to the planning system that exposes the UK to greater relative house price inflation. House price bubbles complicate UK monetary policy. Part of it relates to a tendency to accommodate inflation and a reluctance to take decisions to rein-in economic activity before there is a visibly awkward problem with inflation. Ten years after Margaret Thatcher left office, similar errors in monetary policy were played out again. Too little attention was paid to monetary indicators and measures of bank lending. An asset price bubble in the housing market was ignored. The Monetary Policy Committee was intent on ensuring that the economy continuously expanded at its perceived trend rate of growth, with little unused spare capacity, and its estimate of the trend rate of growth was on the optimistic side.

Margaret Thatcher can be criticised for three things in relation to monetary policy. She was often awkward about raising interest rates. She was reluctant to increase them because of the impact that they had on mortgages. Her attachment to mortgage interest relief aggravated the house price dimension that makes the conduct of UK monetary policy more complicated. And while she expressed periodic concern about the growth of bank lending and the money supply, she was also in charge of a government that after the big disinflation of the early 1980s, was reluctant to bear short-term costs to make further progress in lowering inflation.

Yet that should not obscure the huge achievement in getting inflation down between 1979 and 1983 and the determination exhibited by the Prime Minister and the Chancellor, Nigel Lawson, in correcting the mistakes of the Lawson boom. When Nigel Lawson set interest rates at 15 per cent, it was a measure of the determination to get inflation back down to something below 4 per cent. This was a complete break with what had gone on in the 1970s and 1960s. There may have been mistakes in monetary policy, but the willingness to establish non-accommodating monetary policies and to use very high real interest rates, if necessary, transformed the UK's performance when compared to the legacy of the Radcliffe Committee and the financial chaos of the 1970s.

The policies pursued with great vigour to improve the micro-economic functioning of the economy led to a significant improvement in economic performance. Many micro-economic measures were taken to improve the supply performance of the economy. These included increased product market competition, the withdrawal of industrial subsidies, denationalisation, exposing the newly privatised industries to greater competition, and subjecting privatised companies that enjoyed monopoly power to a proper regulatory framework. Labour market incentives were improved as a result of the end of incomes policy, changes to industrial relations, and trade union law. The benefits system was restructured to improve job searching by testing availability for work more effectively and introducing the actively seeking work test and lowering the replacement ratio of out-of-work benefits to wages.

Over the life of the Thatcher governments, economic policy evolved into a systematic attempt to improve the supply performance of the economy. In many instances it was about measures intended to remove barriers that impeded markets from working. At the heart of the programme was the creation of more competition in domestic markets and exposing producers to international competition so that the economy as a whole was more open and more contested. It was a series of micro-economic measures that cohered into a substantial improvement in the supply side of the UK economic. Its purpose was to improve the living standards and economic welfare of the residents living and working in the UK. But it did not go unnoticed by the rest of the world. The UK became very attractive to international investors and began to attract a disproportionate amount of inward investment into the EU.

The best way of assessing the overall impact of the Thatcher economic legacy is to look at how the UK economy has performed compared to other major mature economies. This is better than comparing growth rates of GDP before and after 1979, because all the major advanced economies have shared challenges and enjoyed opportunities that are very different from those prevailing before the 1970s. Among them are the much greater cost of oil and a huge increase in international competition, along with changes in computers and technology that combine to have complex implications for earnings and employment.

This means that assessing the economic benefits of the Thatcher programme, in terms of whether GDP growth was marginally faster or slower post-Thatcher, is misleading and simplistic. Many of Margaret Thatcher's critics fall into this error.

Professor John Van Reenen, the Director of the Centre for Economic Performance at the London School of Economics, has looked at the economic legacy and concluded that 'there is a substantial body of evidence suggesting that a range of important policy changes initiated by her underpinned these economic gains', which were an economic revival spurred on by supply-side policies that enabled the UK to catch up with the living standards of other developed economies, having fallen behind them in terms of material well-being. Professor Van Reenen is not in any way a *parti pris* Thatcherite. He is a member of the board of the Fabian Society and a former adviser to the last Labour Government and he admits that as 'a student I was not a fan of her Government, but in retrospect I believe it is clear that the important changes in economic policies that began at the end of the 1970s contributed to the reversal of a century of UK relative economic decline.'

While the UK continued to enjoy significant improvements in living standards in the 200 years following the Industrial Revolution, UK GDP per capita began from 1870 to decline relative to that in France, Germany and the USA. Much of this relative decline was inevitable as other countries caught up with the technical lead that Britain had once enjoyed and created institutional settings that supported the accumulation and use of capital that were better than those in Britain for much of the 20th century. Van Reenen shows that by the 1970s, US GDP per capita was 40 per cent higher than in the UK and in the major European economies such as West Germany and France it was 10 to 15 per cent higher. Thirty years later, Van Reenen shows that the UK's relative performance has substantially improved. By 2007, before the credit crunch and the Great Recession, UK GDP per capita had overtaken that of both France and Germany and significantly reduced the gap with the US.

Between 1950 and 1980 UK GDP per capita fell relative to that in France, Germany and the US, but it started to increase relative to them after 1980s. Moreover, Van Reenen points out that this continues to be true even when the data is taken up to the Great Recession after 2008. This improvement in relative economic performance has been driven by a better labour market where more people are in jobs and improvements in productivity have been achieved. Van Reenen shows that GDP per UK worker has risen since 1979 and continues to be 'impressive even taking the crisis into consideration. Unemployment since 2008 has been much lower than would have been expected given the fall in output'.

Van Reenen makes the point that these improvements in performance were not the misleading artefact of an economy dominated by finance and inflated in a bubble. The productivity improvement was spread across industrial sectors. Finance had only contributed 10 per cent of the productivity growth since 1979. Van Reenen's conclusion is that 'the supply side reforms were no illusion'.

Professor Nicholas Crafts of Warwick University shares Van Reenen's view that that relative performance of the UK economy improved under Margaret Thatcher. The productivity gap between the UK and Germany and France narrowed and real GDP per capita in the UK over took that in Germany and France. Crafts emphasises the manner in which open and contested markets raised productivity. There was greater pressure on management to perform. Liberalisation of capital markets facilitated divestment and restructuring in large firms. Management buyouts, often financed through private equity, generated large increases in total factor productivity. Privatisation raised productivity in the nationalised industries, particularly in the period when they were being prepared for sale. More competitive product markets meant that productivity had to be improved. Even in manufacturing sectors where trade union power was visibly entrenched there were fewer monopoly profits to be shared, with the result that productivity was raised.

Deregulation and more open and competitive markets enabled firms to make greater use of IT and technology. Technology offers much greater opportunities to raise productivity and profits if businesses can reorganise their management and working practices. Crafts points out that this 'would not have happened with 1970s style industrial relations'. New technology, plant and equipment have little impact on either productivity or profits if the unions have an effective veto over its use and deployment. Crafts highlights the notorious example of the old newspaper industry in Fleet Street. An investment of £50 million could have saved the newspapers £35 million a year, but such technical innovation was blocked by the print unions, until the showdown between Rupert Murdoch and the print workers over working practices at News International. The dock industry had shown that even transforming technologies such as containerisation cannot be properly used in the face of an effective union veto of the sort provided through the Dock Labour Scheme. Crafts' judgement is that productivity was boosted by the interaction of reforms to industrial relations and product-market competition.

That does not mean that Van Reenen offers an unreserved endorsement of Thatcher's legacy. He criticises the growth of inequality both in terms of pre-tax incomes, and through changes made to the tax system that benefited higher income households. The Gini coefficient increased by nine percentage points in the 1980s. Margaret Thatcher was not an egalitarian. Part of her critique of the post-war Keynesian welfare consensus was that the redistribution of income and wealth had gone too far and success and enterprise were not properly rewarded. Indeed, incentives and profits in the 1970s were so squeezed that a market economy could not function properly. What she offered and delivered was a market economy where there would be incentives that would reward education, talent, enterprise and hard work. An inevitable artefact of a market economy is a wide dispersion of income and wealth and one that was likely to be wider than that exhibited in the mixed economy of the 1970s. Margaret Thatcher recognised this and spelled out what she meant in the provocative speech she made in New York in 1975. As Nicholas Crafts puts it: 'the Thatcher experiment was about making a liberal market economy work better.' There is a trade off between efficiency and equality. Margaret Thatcher placed an emphasis on efficiency to ensure that there was more economic growth and higher GDP per head.

That does not mean that she was responsible for, or approved of, the kind of rent-seeking by senior company executives that has been exhibited over the last 15 years. And nor is it consistent with a properly functioning market economy. The problem she faced in the 1970s was senior managers in the private and public sector industries who encountered difficult obstacles when carrying out basic managerial functions and were offered limited rewards when they overcame those obstacles. While the contemporary rent-seeking by company directors needs to be curbed, that does not mean that a return to the kind of incentives and pay differentials of the 1960s and 1970s would be appropriate.

Chapter 23: Alternatives to Thatcher in the Early 1980s

THERE ARE SOME PEOPLE WHO ARGUE that the things that Margaret Thatcher accomplished would have happened anyway. Moreover, they go on to say that, while the changes were necessary, they could have been accomplished in a gentler and more emollient manner that would have avoided both a great deal of economic and social distress as well as a lot of political bitterness. The changes that Margaret Thatcher brought about that many of those critics now regard as necessary, could not have been implemented without a high degree of contention. There were also heavy and unavoidable transition costs. The reason why the changes were needed is that governments for a generation had generally avoided making them and when they did attempt to do so they resiled in the face of intense political opposition.

It is worth examining the alternative economic policies on offer in the early 1980s. In 1979 the Labour Government of James Callaghan offered not so much a manifesto as a commentary on what had gone wrong and how they could do better. The 1978 White Paper on the nationalised industries was a catalogue of how not to do it. Eric Varley, the Secretary of State for Industry, had developed a policy of selective assistance to help modernise British industry that was principally predicated on avoiding all the previous mistakes – the Industrial Reorganisation Committee of Lord Kearton, the picking winners and the failed workers co-operatives of Meriden and Kirby. There was no attempt to consider structural reform of the labour market, reform of the trade unions, or institutions such as the Dock Labour Scheme. In fact, the commitment to implement the recommendations of Lord Bullock's report on industrial democracy would have further entrenched trade union power. In firms employing over 2,000 employees, trade union member-nominated board members would have had a direct role with regard to management appointments, a firm's capital structure, use of resources and dividend payments. Lord Bullock's proposals would have extended many of the defects of the Dock Labour Act to most large UK companies.

In 1981 the Labour Party, that had moved radically to the left in the 1970s, divided. A significant minority of 'social democrat' moderate-minded Labour MPs and Members of the House of Lords formed the Social Democrat Party (SDP) and entered into an electoral alliance with the Liberal Party. The SDP-Liberal Alliance's programme was never very clear. Despite being led by a former Labour Chancellor of the Exchequer, Roy Jenkins, who had presided over a brief period of effective disinflation following the 1967 devaluation, the Alliance's economic policies remained, at best, an urbane fudge. It appeared to offer a mild reflation, additional public investment, minor social and economic reforms and a modest devaluation of the pound. As the Cambridge economist Robert Rowthorn commented in *Marxism Today*, it was 'merely a half-speed version of the Barber 'dash for growth' of 1972-73'.

Michael Bleaney, a contributor to *Marxism Today*, identified Conservative economic policy as 'an unusually energetic and forthright expression of the class interests of British capital through a sustained onslaught on the trade union movement and the public sector'. Bleaney saw it as a strategy based on low wages, combined with an experienced workforce to attract investment which would otherwise have gone elsewhere in the EEC. Deflation was an integral part of the strategy. This Marxist analysis saw the programme of the Thatcher Government 'as a considered and highly dangerous and unusual mobilisation of the total resources of the ruling class in order to effect a permanent shift in the balance of class forces in Britain'. The Marxist view of Thatcherite economics was a form of repugnance tempered by intellectual respect. The contributors to *Marxism Today* understood what many of the social democrat critics of the Conservative Government's programme failed to recognise: that it amounted to a serious and systematic attempt to reconstruct a market economy that could perform.

The problem for the Government as perceived by this Marxian analysis was not that the economic strategy was flawed, incoherent or mistaken, but it may not have had the political time for the strategy to work. The crash, the clearing away of failed companies and the development of new dynamic enterprises to replace them may have taken too long to avoid either a U-turn or electoral defeat. They did not doubt the necessity of the policies if an effective market economy were to be revived.

The real alternative to Margaret Thatcher's programme was the Alternative Economic Strategy and New Cambridge. As my own economics tutor, Walter Eltis, told me when I asked what would happen if the Government's programme failed, 'then I suppose, we would have to try New Cambridge'. The Department of Applied Economics at Cambridge under the direction of Wynne Godley developed a critique of the British Keynesian consensus on economic policy. Much of the debate generated by New Cambridge was recondite, concerning the stability of the private sector's accumulation of financial assets, and the role of budget and fiscal policy in stabilising the balance of payments, but it united a policy agenda that sought to square full employment and sustained economic growth with a balance of payments protected by import controls. Most of the debate was conducted within a conventional Keynesian national accounting framework, but it attracted economists and politicians who had a Marxian agenda where private business and private property rights would be treated in a more contingent and confining way than they had been at any time since the economic controls imposed during the Second World War. As Nigel Lawson put it in a speech in 1980, if there was an alternative, it was 'a bastard form of Keynesianism that is in reality closer to central planning and the command economy, and is scarcely a recognisable variant of Keynesian at all.'

In some iterations, the AES was an expansion of domestic demand with the balance of payments crudely buttressed by import controls; in others it was presented as a more nuanced concept of managed trade. A group of economists led by Lord Currie contributed to the AES by offering policies based on planning imports, with an extension of democratic planning and control to major areas of the economy. They planned not to reduce imports, but to expand demand and prevent the level of imports from rising. It was not therefore a demand for protection, but a demand for management of trade. Such a policy was difficult because of the threat of trade retaliation. This was a serious problem for the UK because of its dependence on exports. UK innovation was weak and it had to import technology whether by foreign imports or direct ownership.

The thought that went into the AES strongly influenced the Labour manifesto *New Hope for Britain* in 1983. Although it is now amusingly referred to as the longest suicide note in history and is credited with contributing to Michael Foot's massive defeat, it offered a coherent, if unattractive, alternative to Margaret Thatcher's programme. The programme included an £11 billion emergency action programme of fiscal reflation, equivalent to about 3.6 per cent of GDP; a five-year plan; controls and direction of bank lending, with plans to nationalise the banks if they did not co-operate in full with plan; renationalisation of BT, British Aerospace and the British Shipbuilding Corporation; import controls to protect key industries; foreign exchange controls and an annual wealth tax. It was Labour's official programme and it was the alternative that was being offered. How workable it would have been is not clear, although it is possible to surmise from the experience of France between 1981 and 1983 that it would have had to be abandoned.

Alternatives to Thatcher in the Early 1980s

Chapter 24: France's *Programme Common*: Neo-Keynesian Economics in One Country

WHEN FRANÇOIS MITTERRAND WAS ELECTED in May 1981, Michael Foot greeted it on the BBC's *Panorama* programme as a hugely exciting event and looked forward to seeing the joint Socialist-Communist *Programme Common* being implemented. François Mitterrand applied a neo-Keynesian programme of economic expansion to expedite the recovery of the sluggish French economy he had inherited from Valéry Giscard d'Estaing. Its purpose was to insulate France from the international recession. These policies resulted in rapid and strong growth in private domestic consumption and sustained inflation. Transfer payments and the minimum wage were increased and working hours were reduced. This increased social spending was only partly financed through higher taxation and a new wealth tax. The government budget balance swung from a surplus of 0.3 per cent of GDP in 1980 to deficits of 1.6 per cent in 1981 and 2.9 per cent in 1982. Monetary policy accommodated this fiscal expansion. Domestic credit expanded by 16 per cent in 1981 and 1982. There was a sharp monetisation of the budget deficit, with lending to the government sector rising by 22 per cent in 1982 and 23 in 1981.

An economic expansion fuelled by consumption, where investment stagnated resulted in a severe balance of payments problem, aggravated by entrenched high inflation relative to other economies. As world commodity prices fell, French inflation fell, but not by as much as in other countries. Despite attempts by government ministers to talk down wage growth, domestic wages increased in double digits and the growth rate of real wages roughly doubled. This resulted in the French rate of unemployment rising from 6.3 per cent in 1980 to 8.6 per cent in 1982. Higher employment costs and higher wages resulted in a decline of company profits. The French current account deteriorated sharply from a deficit of $4.2 billion in 1980 to $12.1 billion in 1982. Imports rose in volume terms by 2.4 per cent and exports fell by 3.5 per cent. The weakness in export volumes was not simply the result of weak international markets, but strong domestic markets that diverted output from the exporting traded goods sector. There were sharp outflows of private capital and there was heavy French official borrowing from abroad, with net officially authorised borrowing trebling to almost $12 billion a year in 1982.

This resulted in growing concern about France's accumulating external debt and the stability of the franc within the European Monetary System (EMS). The combination of relatively high inflation, rising unemployment, a progressively less competitive manufacturing sector, a haemorrhaging balance of payments position aggravated by an exchange rate constrained by the EMS, was by any criterion an awkward mix that could not be sustained. France devalued twice within the EMS at this stage. These realignments – devaluations against the Deutschmark – offset France's adverse inflation performance, but they were not accompanied by the necessary fiscal measures needed to curtail domestic spending on consumption.

This led to a third devaluation in March 1983. This was coupled with a severe domestic austerity package. Discretionary increases in taxes and cuts in spending equivalent to 2 per cent of GDP were announced. The measures focused on cutting domestic consumption spending and induced an unpredicted squeeze in real consumer spending. Social Security taxes were increased by a surcharge of 1 per cent, excise duties were raised and monetary conditions were tightened, with tough lower targets for both monetary and credit growth. This ended the experiment with neo-Keynesian demand management in one country. An open international economy could not sustain an expansion of domestic demand, because of the vulnerability of its balance of payments. Moreover structural rigidities in the labour market meant that, far from experiencing a reduction in the rate of unemployment, the labour market deteriorated. The only way the policy could have been sustained would have been to erect protectionist barriers to shut out imports. That would have further distorted the French economy and diverted resources to inefficient industries. It would have triggered retaliation that would have lowered French exports Given that exports of goods and services accounted for about a third of GDP, such protection would have hurt France.

France then embarked on a policy of macro-economic monetary and fiscal caution supervised by its Finance Minister, Jacques Delors. Over the next seven years a policy that became known as the 'franc fort' transformed France into Europe's strongest financial economy. France in effect attempted to outbid Germany in terms of monetary stringency. The authors of the *Programme Common* would never have expected that their Socialist agenda would have dissolved into such a stringent version of financial orthodoxy. Orthodox monetary policies based on adhering tightly to German monetary conditions within the framework of the ERM delivered low inflation and a strong balance of payments surplus. High public expenditure and taxation along with inflexible labour and product market regulation resulted in disappointing economic growth and rising structural unemployment. France systematically made micro-economic policy mistakes that damaged employment, living standards and economic growth.

Whatever else the *Programme Common* may have been, it is was not an encouraging advertisement for the ideas and analysis that lay behind much of the Alternative Economic Strategy in the UK. It failed in its own terms and had to be abandoned. The leakages of increased demand through the growth of imports and the impracticality of import protection without retaliation exposed the impracticality of conventional Keynesian demand management in one country. It led the more thoughtful supporters of the AES, who remained committed to its analysis, to recognise that it could only work in the context of international co-ordination. Dr Stuart Holland is a good example of such an economist. Dr Holland had been Tony Benn's special adviser at the Department of Trade and Industry and was later the Labour MP for Vauxhall. This contributed to the change in the Left's attitude to Europe. European integration was embraced partly because of the potential opportunities that it offered for co-ordinated trans-continental economic expansion. In the second half of the 1980s the Labour Party became a committed supporter of the UK participation in the ERM, although it asserted that it would remove what its policy documents such as *Meet the Challenge – Make the Change* in 1989 called its deflationary bias. Labour was also encouraged to embrace Europe's social agenda by the provocative speech of the President of the European Commission, Jacques Delors, to the TUC Congress at Brighton in 1988. While some of the EU's micro-economic and social policies may have been superficially attractive to the British Left, the macro-economic orthodoxy transmitted through the European Commission, the Bundesbank and preparations for the single currency, were completely at odds with its nostalgic interest in neo-Keynesian economics.

Chapter 25: Margaret Thatcher and Europe

PART OF THE LABOUR PARTY'S EMBRACING OF EUROPE in the late 1980s was an atavistic response to Margaret Thatcher's increasing reservations about European integration. This scepticism about the EU was expressed in her speech to the College of Europe in Bruges in 1988, where she explained that she had not rolled back the state in Britain only to have it reintroduced by the back door through processes of European integration.

Initially a conventional pragmatic pro-European party leader

SUPERFICIALLY, MARGARET THATCHER CAN BE SEEN as a pragmatic British Prime Minister who in practice worked within the constraints of the European treaties and policies, until her distaste for them made her a vocal and disruptive critic. As Leader of the Conservative Party, in Opposition and as Prime Minister, Margaret Thatcher was a conventional late 20th century party leader in the same mould as Harold Wilson, James Callaghan and John Major. As Leader of the Opposition, having served in Ted Heath's Cabinet when the UK joined in 1973, she backed the Yes campaign in the 1975 referendum to stay in the EEC. The Conservative Party led by her remained pro-European. When the EMS was created in 1979, she condemned James Callaghan for keeping sterling out of its exchange rate mechanism, arguing that it was Labour's failed economic policies that prevented sterling from joining.

A flair for performing on the stage and attracting attention but limited influence

IN HIS 1979 VALEDICTORY DISPATCH, Nicholas Henderson, the retiring British ambassador to France, recognised that President Giscard d'Estaing 'is not really very interested in us at the moment and gives the impression that Anglo/French relations only feature in his mind when the annual Summit comes along'. That changed with Margaret Thatcher. She cut a startling and vivid figure at European Council Meetings. She was never anything other than centre stage, even when the UK was alone in matters, such as negotiations over the UK net contribution to the EEC Budget. This had a lot to do with her personality and political style, but it also reflected the perception that she was a serious politician trying to carry through significant structural changes to deal with the UK's long-term economic problems. As the UK became more economically successful her international stature increased.

Awkward personal relationships with European leaders

MARGARET THATCHER DID NOT GET ON WELL with other European leaders. Unlike American politicians, she made little effort to build enduring and effective personal relationships with them. In many instances there were fundamental differences of philosophy that inevitably stood in the way. There would always be a limit to the extent to which Margaret Thatcher would reach agreement with a socialist, social democrat or corporatist Christian Democrat on the details of domestic economic policy, from farming to employment law.

Things were not helped by the difficult relationship that the Prime Minister had with the German Chancellor, Helmut Kohl. Dr Kohl was a conservative Christian Democrat who should in principle have been a politician with whom she could have been able to find common ground. Yet her relationship with him was cool, if not frosty. A better personal relationship would probably have helped, but the extent to which a greater rapport would really have changed anything should not be exaggerated. On many of the contentious matters such as agriculture and employment Dr Kohl and his German Christian Social union had a fundamentally different outlook. As the single market was being developed in the late 1980s, the German government wanted a series of European directives to increase the costs of production in low wage economies such as Spain and Portugal to prevent what the labour attaché at the German Embassy in London called 'social dumping'.

German reunification in 1990

IN 1990 AFTER THE FALL OF THE BERLIN Wall the reunification of Germany came on to the international political agenda for the first time since the creation of the two German states in the 1940s. Although diplomatically and militarily impractical, it had been UK and US policy since 1945, and it was a major West German preoccupation. Margaret Thatcher had serious reservations about a united Germany being dangerous and too powerful. Initially she and President Mitterrand shared these concerns and egged each other on in holding onto (at best outdated) prejudices. There was a remarkable exchange between President Mitterrand and Margaret Thatcher at the regular Anglo/French summit held on one occasion at Waddesden Manor in Buckinghamshire. After reading the transcript, Mrs Judith Chaplin, one of the special advisers at the Treasury, commented that it was like reading a conversation between two old-age pensioners, each provoking the other into denouncing the Germans. As part of Thatcher's analysis of what German unification might imply, she convened a seminar of distinguished historians who disabused her of her prejudices. Margaret Thatcher was not alone in having reservations about German unification. The elderly socialist President of Italy in the 1980s denounced German unity and President Mitterrand was initially happy to share Margaret Thatcher's prejudices. Yet there is no doubt that her stance on German unification was a mistake that damaged her. The combination of being wrong, unable to do anything to stop it, being out of step with American President George Bush, and further alienating the German Chancellor Dr Kohl was a significant error.

Fontainebleau Agreement 1984: getting Britain's money back

THE EARLY YEARS OF HER PERIOD IN OFFICE, in terms of Europe, were taken up with a protracted argument over the UK's net contribution to the EEC Budget. About 80 per cent of the EEC Budget was absorbed by spending on the Common Agricultural Policy (CAP). The UK, with a small agricultural sector, received little from it, yet through the contribution made from VAT receipts, ended up being the largest net contributor to the Budget, despite the fact that the UK was the second poorest member of the EEC in the early 1980s. Margaret Thatcher demanded that Britain should be given its money back. Foreign Office advice was that little progress would be made with the campaign and that her direct and intemperate *modus operandi* would in any case be counter-productive. Margaret Thatcher, however, got her way at the Fontainebleau

Summit in 1984, because, as Nigel Lawson has pointed out, she threatened to withhold the UK's Budget contribution. The Fontainebleau Agreement rebates two-thirds of the net UK's contribution to the Budget. Since 1985 the Fontainebleau abatement has saved on average 3.6 billion euros a year and cumulatively almost 100 billion euros.

Although from the mid-1980s the Prime Minister opposed sterling's participation in the ERM when Nigel Lawson first started to suggest it, her Government remained pro–European, leading the way on the creation of the Single European Market and supporting the Single European Act with its expedited procedures of qualified majority voting to enable measures necessary to complete the market to be passed more easily. She appointed UK Commissioners who were strong pro-Europeans such as Lord Cockfield and Leon Brittan, who played a significant role in creating the agenda that led to the single market.

Chapter 26: The French Revolution, the European Social Charter and the Paris Summit 1989

SUPERFICIALLY, MARGARET THATCHER GOT ON QUITE WELL with François Mitterrand, the socialist president of France. At the height of the Cold War, President Mitterrand ensured that France was a strong military supporter of the Western alliance and was much more co-operative with NATO than his Gaullist predecessors had been. Moreover, in the darkest moments during the Falklands War French military co-operation had been very helpful to the UK. Things were helped by the fact that Margaret Thatcher found him interesting and enjoyed his company. Yet there does not appear to be much love lost between them. President Mitterrand and his advisers ensured that there was plenty of barbed, if not vitriolic, briefing about Margaret Thatcher that was effective in being diminishing of her personally.

In 1988 Margaret Thatcher began to have significant reservations about European integration. There was accumulating evidence that the Single European Act and the qualified majority voting procedure was being abused by the European Commission to pass directives that were not strictly necessary for the completion of the single market. Jacques Delors' speech to the TUC predicting that 80 per cent of all future social and economic legislation would originate from Brussels provoked and worried the Prime Minister. Delors and Mitterrand had the idea of producing a European Social Charter (accompanied by a European Social Action Programme of 20 directives drafted by the Social Affairs Commissioner Mrs Papandreou) to be agreed at the European Council held to mark the bicentenary of the French Revolution. It was to match the French Revolution's *Declaration of the Rights of Man* and to give a social dimension to the single market. The British Government responded by arguing that the social dimension of the single market was the jobs and income that would be generated by properly functioning competitive product markets. Intense efforts were made to get the British Government to drop its opposition to the Social Charter. At one stage Leon Brittan was regularly telephoning Norman Fowler, the Secretary of State for Employment, to try and get him to drop his opposition to it. At her request, the weekend before the launch of the Conservative European Election manifesto in 1989, a briefing note on the legal basis of the proposed charter and its consequences was produced by the Department of Employment. The legal advice was provided by an experienced government lawyer, who had recently moved from heading the section of the Treasury Solicitors in charge of EC litigation. Hugh Purse was a careful and good lawyer, who could lucidly explain complex law, and how courts and tribunals in practice made decisions. The note made the point that the Treaty of Rome was a dynamic legal document, that European Court of Justice tended to expand the legal competence of EC institutions, and that if the EC issued a charter of social ambitions, the Court would probably ensure that its institutions would be given the means to give effect to them. In practice, it could mean directives being tabled on qualified majority voting procedures, which by the letter of the treaties would appear to be unlawful, but the European Court of Justice would accommodate a loose interpretation of the Treaty. He gave the example of the litigation surrounding the Erasmus programme. This was very different from the highly nuanced advice that the Prime Minister normally received from the Foreign Office, the Cabinet Office and the law officers, that was coached in the careful language of what Hugo Young called 'mendacious reassurance'. The Prime Minster was very angry and denounced the charter as 'Marxism', which it plainly was not.

She went to Paris and did a pretty good job of spoiling the party atmosphere surrounding the celebration of the French Revolution She gave a televised interview to *Libération* in Downing Street before she left for Paris. When asked if she thought the Revolution was the basis of Britain's freedom and democracy, she denounced it and said that, if anything, it put back freedom, democracy and the rule of law. This caused outrage and consternation. However, in an article in *The New York Review of Books* about a year later reviewing the *Harvard Encyclopaedia* account of the French Revolution, Conor Cruise O'Brien examined her assertions and broadly vindicated them. He pointed out that President Mitterrand had constructed a sugary 'pastoral' account of the Revolution that was historically highly misleading, and that the only international leader present in Paris who refused to go along in a polite manner with this travesty was Margaret Thatcher. In O'Brien's view this made for a spectacular piece of showbusiness that placed the Revolution at the centre of the evolution of human rights throughout the world. This version of events brushed out the violence of the terror, the invasion and imposition of French revolutionary power on France's European neighbours, and the authoritarian reaction it provoked in other countries that had been more liberal than the French *ancien régime*. It is worth looking at what O'Brien wrote:

'The organizers of the bicentenary celebrations came up with a brilliant answer to that one. The answer is that the French Revolution is at the centre of the history of liberty and human rights in the world. The theme of the spectacular parade that rolled down the Champs Elysées on the night of July 14, 1989, was essentially that of Frédéric Auguste Bartholdi's

governing concept for his Statue of Liberty: La Liberté éclairant le monde.

Now this made a very satisfactory answer, both politically and as show biz. Politically, by deflecting attention away from the actual course of the Revolution into the idea of the Revolution, it cleared up the Revolution conceptually, and made it into an acceptable and domesticated heritage for the modern, centrist Socialist party. The actual course of the Revolution was bloody, divisive, disconcerting, and generally scary: associations which any modern French socialist wishes to keep well away from. But the idea of the French Revolution in the minds of foreign admirers can be as nice as you choose to make it. It would be hard to think of a more effective way of sanitizing a sanguinary political heritage. Knowing their business, the organizers of the agreeable version of pastoral enacted in Paris last July did not introduce the concepts of French Revolutionary expansion, or of la Grande Nation. Instead, the celebrations hinged on a sacred document, *the* Declaration of the Rights of Man and of the Citizen *proclaimed by the National Assembly in April 1789.* To this document, it was suggested, humanity everywhere owes such freedom as it has been able to achieve, and the hope of freedom in the places where freedom today has not yet been achieved. Various foreign intellectuals were there, on that magical July night in Paris, solemnly confirming over television the transcendent significance in universal history of the document which constituted the clou of François Mitterrand's triumphant Version of Pastoral. Margaret Thatcher was also in Paris that night, but in quite a different mood. She felt she had been brought to Paris on false pretences, and had then had a false role thrust on her. Mitterrand, as well as being president of France, happened to be president of the European Community at the time, and he had called a European summit to coincide with the bicentenary celebration. By this masterly move, he co-opted the other European leaders into walk-on roles – in his Version of Pastoral. By attending a part of the celebrations – as common courtesy required them to do – they appeared to be giving mute confirmation to the governing concept of the bicentenary: that other nations owe their freedom to the French.

The other European leaders, with one exception, meekly accepted their *roles as spear carriers in a Franco-centric pageant. Mrs Thatcher, however, broke the spell. British freedom, she affirmed, owed nothing to a French document of the late eighteenth century. British freedom rested on ancient and native foundations. It went back to Magna Carta.*

This was strongly felt to be in the worst of taste. But let us now look at the Declaration of the Rights of Man and of the Citizen, *with some assistance from the* Critical Dictionary *entry, "Rights of Man," by Marcel Gauchet. The Declaration owes nothing directly to the Magna Carta. The authors of the Declaration would have been horrified at the very thought that it might. "The thirteenth century? Ugh!" Yet the Declaration does owe a very great deal to the Anglo-Saxon (more properly here, Anglo-Norman) tradition of freedom, of which Magna Carta is a conspicuous part. That tradition in the early eighteenth century reached the French Enlightenment from England itself. (Voltaire was the most enthusiastic importer of English ideas of freedom.) By the late eighteenth century, however, it was from America that the French Revolution imported the Anglo-Saxon tradition.'*

This episode illustrates a feature of Margaret Thatcher's public life that was repeated in several instances. She was serious and unafraid to challenge conventional pieties. She often did so in a slightly clumsy manner, but was usually more right than she was wrong. And her intellectual interest and political willingness to take risks to do so was in marked contrast to most politicians in this country and abroad.

Margaret Thatcher then went to join the Summit where she vetoed the European Social Charter. It was also the European Council that received the report of experts chaired by Jacques Delors, proposing the creation of a European Single Currency. The Prime Minister made it clear that the UK would not be taking part in it. By that stage she was not just isolated within Europe, but increasingly isolated within the British establishment and wider political elite.

The French Revolution, the European Social Charter and the Paris Summit 1989

Chapter 27: Europe's Role in Margaret Thatcher's Downfall, Sovereignty and the Future of Europe

WHILE MARGARET THATCHER was developing a Gaullist critique of the EC and the role of the Commission, and expressing her hostility to the proposed European currency, she was at the same time, albeit it reluctantly, agreeing to allow sterling to enter the ERM. Her instincts on European integration were similar to those of the French President, Charles de Gaulle. She was against supranational agencies and wanted to preserve the effective sovereignty of the nation state. Her preferred institution for EU cooperation was the Council of Ministers, rather than the European Parliament or European Commission, with decisions ideally being taken on the basis of unanimity. This illustrates how, although her rhetoric had become hostile to the federal European project, she in practice – given the political constraints she operated within – pragmatically accommodated further engagement with Europe. On 30 October 1990, following the European Council meeting that approved the preparations for the two intergovernmental conferences on economic and monetary union and also on institutional reform that went on to become the Maastricht Treaty establishing the single currency in a statement to the House of Commons, the Prime Minister said :

> 'On economic and monetary union, I stressed that we would be ready to move beyond the present position to the creation of a European monetary fund and a common Community currency which we have called a hard Ecu. But we would not be prepared to agree to set a date for starting the next stage of economic and monetary union before there is any agreement on what that stage should comprise. And I again emphasised that we would not be prepared to have a single currency imposed upon us, nor to surrender the use of the pound sterling as our currency.
>
> The hard Ecu would be a parallel currency, not a single currency. If, as time went by, people and governments chose to use it widely, it could evolve towards a single currency. But our national currency would remain unless a decision to abolish it were freely taken by future generations of Parliament and people. A single currency is not the policy of this Government.
>
> I should like to offer four comments in conclusion. Britain intends to be part of the further political, economic and monetary development of the European Community. That is what the great majority of member states want, too. When we come to negotiate on particular points, rather than concepts or generalities, I believe that solutions will be found which will enable the Community to go forward as Twelve'.

In answer to an effectively provocative question from the Leader of the Opposition, Neil Kinnock, Margaret Thatcher expressed her gut feelings about Europe:

> 'Yes, the Commission wants to increase its powers. Yes, it is a non-elected body and I do not want the Commission to increase its powers at the expense of the House, so of course we differ. The President of the Commission, Mr Delors, said at a press conference the other day that he wanted the European Parliament to be the democratic body of the Community, he

wanted the Commission to be the Executive and he wanted the Council of Ministers to be the Senate. No. No. No'.

These trenchantly expressed views contributed to the determination of her senior Cabinet colleagues to remove her from office. This statement played a significant part in provoking Sir Geoffrey Howe, her long-serving Foreign Secretary, who was very pro-European, to resign. He had been Chancellor in her first administration when inflation was brought down decisively. Margaret Thatcher had removed him from the Foreign Office in 1989. This was as a punishment for joining with Nigel Lawson, the Chancellor, to force her into agreeing to the 'Madrid conditions' for sterling's entry into the ERM. He became the Lord President of the Council and Leader of the House of Commons and was given the 'Pooh Bah' position of Deputy Prime Minister. Sir Geoffrey became the leader of the internal opposition within the Government to the Prime Minister's European policy. It was this "No, No, No" statement, and the complete isolation of the British Prime Minister at the Rome Council that caused him to resign. Relations between Margaret Thatcher and Sir Geoffrey were not helped by the Prime Minister being rude to him over some mess-up related to the forthcoming legislative programme. Margaret Thatcher's attitude to Europe and her manner with senior colleagues contributed to her downfall, when Michael Heseltine challenged her in an internal leadership election a few weeks later in November 1990. Disagreement over Europe and the ERM were central to the resignations of both Nigel Lawson and Geoffrey Howe. Both resignations made her politically vulnerable. While Margaret Thatcher's instincts and prejudices on Europe were plain, it should be noted that her actions remained much more nuanced and pragmatic, even at the end. She had, moreover, only just agreed to sterling entering the ERM a few weeks earlier in September 1990.

The debate surrounding the UK's future in the EU

MARGARET THATCHER'S EUROPEAN LEGACY is not so much what she did in government, as the public debate that she helped to frame about European integration in the years ahead. The purpose of the Bruges speech in 1988 was to shift British policy on European integration and to move the Conservative Party away from the official pro-European position it had occupied since the mid-1960s. Its initial effect was to isolate her among European heads of government and to make her vulnerable within the political elite in the Conservative Party in government and in Parliament. But it galvanised the Conservative Party into a radical debate about the future of Europe. Until the Bruges speech and her provocative commentary on Europe, opponents of European integration were a small and politically irrelevant rump of opponents of the old Common Market. They were mainly elderly, usually maverick, and often interesting individuals, who politically counted for nought. Margaret Thatcher changed that. She initiated a debate about Europe and in many respects framed its reference points. First, there was the opposition to the single currency, then the critique of the role of the European Commission as a legislative body, followed by the repudiation of the Single European Act and qualified majority voting and with it by implication the single market, and finally in her last active years the rejection of membership itself.

Margaret Thatcher's period in power coincided with a dramatic recovery of impetus in the European project. After the first oil crisis in 1973 and the collapse of the so-called "snake currency" arrangements, the federal European agenda, with its grandiose ambitions for a European economic and monetary policy, appeared to have run into the sand. Anthony Teasdale in *The Penguin Companion to the European Union* shows how Jacques Delors's politically astute leadership as President of the European Commission brought that federal project back to life. Much of it was written into the Treaty of Rome that plainly envisaged a dynamic expansion of the role of Europe's supranational institutions and policies. By emphasising the social dimension of the single market, Delors mobilised political consent for a series of liberalising policies that would override national policy. A clash with politicians in Britain was inevitable, because the Europe that the UK had joined by signing the Treaty of Rome was not the Europe described by the then Prime Minister, Edward Heath, in his 1972 White Paper. The British political establishment originally had been reluctant to go along with the European project when it was first promoted in the 1950s, because of these fundamental issues of sovereignty. When that same establishment decided it was expedient to set those concerns aside and join, it pretended to itself that they were no longer genuine problems. And so began what Hugo Young called the 'mendacious reassurance'. By 1988 Margaret Thatcher saw the position for what it was. In the arguments leading to and following the Maastricht Treaty, she was not prepared to pretend that in relation to Europe, the UK was in some kind of Panglossian condition of European multiple geometry where the UK had won all the arguments.

Margaret Thatcher was the first major British politician to break with Europe after the Yes vote in 1975. She paid a high political price for doing so in terms of it contributing to ejecting her from power, although it was by no means the sole reason for her fall. Margaret Thatcher's stance on Europe enabled her to shape the main debate in British politics in three decades that followed her departure from office. The political parties are in broad agreement on most of the domestic and international agenda. The exception is Europe. From 1975 until the mid-2000s, membership of the EU was the basic presumption for all serious politicians, even those with pronounced eurosceptic views. By the time of her death in April 2013 that had changed. Two of the most significant political figures in post-war politics had come out against the UK's continued membership of the EU. Nigel Lawson did so in an interview with the *Financial Times*. Denis Healey took the opportunity of an interview in the *New Statesman* to say so the week before she died. Margaret Thatcher initiated and fundamentally shaped that debate.

Europe's Role in Margaret Thatcher's Downfall, Sovereignty and the Future of Europe

Chapter 28: Conclusion

MARGARET THATCHER CHANGED BRITAIN and changed it for the better. Her economic policies arrested the country's relative economic decline and enabled the UK economy to perform as well, if not better, than other comparable mature advanced economies. She changed the country's sensibility. Modern Britain is a much more meritocratic society as a result of her. Forty years ago, many professionally and financially successful people in middle age still laboured under a sense of social inferiority if they had come from modest social origins or attended a state school. When Margaret Thatcher was accused of being privileged by Denis Healey in the debate on the 1974 finance bill, in a withering reply she pointed out that she had enjoyed no privilege. She made it plain that people should be judged on their merits, not on who their parents were or where they came from. Her close connections with the local Jewish community in her Finchley parliamentary constituency meant that she destroyed the remaining social anti-Semitism in the Conservative Party.

Margaret Thatcher reformed the trade unions and dismantled the mixed economy and the nationalised industries that were at its heart. She extended competition throughout the economy's labour and product markets. Restrictive practices in trade unions were challenged and managements ceased to be protected by a corporatist state. Britain became a more liberal and a less collectivist society.

Margaret Thatcher transformed the UK from a mixed economy into a functioning market economy and systematically took measures that made a market economy work better.

She did not destroy the welfare state. Her policies reformed Social Security benefits and the state second pension in order to make the cost of a welfare state affordable in the context of an aging population – a challenge that the Office for Budget Responsibility has reminded us has not gone away and would be more difficult without the changes made by Margaret Thatcher. The changes made to improve efficiency in the NHS, introducing a purchaser-provider split, creating an internal market and using quasi-markets, have been the basis of serious reform in the NHS in England under Labour, Conservative and Liberal-Democrat ministers.

These changes would not have happened without Margaret Thatcher. The Labour Party in 1980s would not have attempted the agenda of reform that was needed to rectify the UK's emasculated product and labour markets. In 1979 the Labour agenda was about extending trade union power into the boardroom by implementing the TUC's approach to industrial democracy. Revenue from North Sea oil was planned to be used to expand public enterprise through greater investment, rather than any serious attempt to deal with problems of productivity and the low rate of return on existing capital employed in nationalised industries. The interesting question was whether the Left of the Labour Party and the Trade Union movement would get the opportunity to experiment with the Alternative Economic Strategy. A glimpse of what such an adventure would have led to is offered by the first two years of the Mitterrand Government in France and the economic crisis that ended its initial experiment with neo-Keynesianism in 1983.

It is not at all clear that the Macmillan or Heath wing of the Conservative Party that became known as the 'wets' would have pursued an effective agenda of disinflation combined with systematic market reform. Margaret Thatcher was an unusual figure in the Conservative Party. At the top of the Conservative Party in the

1970s she was almost alone. She developed her policies with a small group of sympathetic politicians that went on to dominate Conservative policy-making in government. They included Sir Keith Joseph, Sir Geoffrey Howe, Nigel Lawson, Nicholas Ridley and Norman Tebbit. To suggest that they amounted to a sort of Leninist revolutionary vanguard would be an exaggeration. Yet it is certainly the case that Margaret Thatcher formulated the fundamental policies that shaped her Government against the better judgement and internal opposition of the traditional ministerial elite of the Conservative Party.

Margaret Thatcher broke the post-war, Keynesian collectivist welfare consensus and replaced it with a set of propositions that continue to shape the approach to policy of the Labour and Conservative parties. Price inflation should be contained at something less than around 4 per cent (this is based on what actually happens in terms of action taken rather than what policy or targets may be announced). The public finances should be run so that there is rough balance over the economic cycle, and the stock of public debt should be contained at something no greater than about 40 per cent of national income. Instead of a mixed economy of nationalised industries with a high degree of industrial intervention through subsidy and direct control, combined with an extensive welfare state, there is a market economy with limited industrial intervention and an extensive, but better focused, welfare state. There is a recognition that only so much can be done for a person over his or her lifetime and most individuals have to make a significant contribution to their own welfare in the long term through saving in terms of housing wealth, pensions and other direct savings, such as cash and equities held in Isas. There has been a shift in the balance of taxation from taxation of income and wealth towards expenditure taxes and expenditure tax treatment of savings. The top marginal income tax rate and the basic rate of income tax have fallen by almost a half. In practice, macro-economic policy decisions and important decisions about the tax and benefit system are now taken in a very different manner than they were in the 1970s, whether they are being made by Labour, Conservative or Liberal Democrat ministers.

Ted Heath was elected in 1970 on a radical free-market platform, the Selsdon Manifesto. This promised an end to the support for lame-duck industries, deregulation, and the abolition of statutory prices and incomes policies. Heath failed to carry out the manifesto, and abandoned its central propositions relating to failing industries and prices and wages policy. Rising unemployment resulted in the last full-scale Keynesian reflation when the Prime Minister and his Chancellor, Anthony Barber, went for growth. The Heath Government was an economic failure and a political disaster. Margaret Thatcher succeeded where Ted Heath failed, because of a determination not to be deflected by the short-term vicissitudes of politics and because she had a worked out a coherent alternative policy framework to guide her.

A quarter of a century after Margaret Thatcher left power, the UK has reversed the period of post-war relative economic decline. Much of that can be attributed to improvements in the supply side of the economy. At the heart of those changes was the reform of trade union law that transformed British industrial relations in the private sector. Throughout the 20th century the labour market was the Achilles heel of the British economy, but by the millennium it had become one of its strengths.

Many of these changes were 10 or 20 years overdue. It was an exercise in Schumpeterarian creative destruction. Previous prime ministers had either avoided them, or when they had attempted to make changes to address the problems involved, they either resiled from the political hostility involved, or were defeated by it. Margaret Thatcher's strategy was rooted in the approach of the Roman general Fabius Maximus, who was famous for caution and delay, yet gradually achieved his objectives. She brought huge intelligence and application to everything she did. That application was matched by political vim and vigorous willpower. The combination of having a clear set of policies that she wanted to achieve, a lucid and direct manner of speech and a magisterial purchase on every matter at hand gave her a formidable political authority.

The Maggie Thatcher of folk memory was the product of the intense and sometimes violent political opposition her policies encountered. Previous prime ministers, such as Ted Heath, had been loathed in their time, treated with contempt, and then forgotten. Margaret Thatcher was hated by her enemies because she succeeded where other Conservative politicians had failed. She was one of the most remarkable people to have held the office of Prime Minister. She remains an extraordinary and fascinating figure quite different from most politicians. Almost a quarter of a century after she was ejected from power, Margaret Thatcher is the benchmark that people use to assess contemporary politics, changes in policy, the progress of the economy, and the evolution of British society as a whole.

Conclusion

Bibliography

Nicholas Henderson *Britain's Decline; Its Causes and Consequences* Foreign Office 31 March 1979

Noel Annan *Our Age The Generation that Made Post-War Britain* Fontana 1991

Lord Radcliffe *Committee on the Working of the Monetary System* Cmnd.827 1959

Right Approach to the Economy Conservative Party 1977

Financial Statement and Budget Report 1980-81 1980

Monetary Control Cmnd. 7858 1980

Webbs *History of Trade Unionism* 1920

Nicholas Davenport *The Split Society* Victor Gollancz 1964

Michael Shanks *The Stagnant Society* Pelican Books 1961

Lord Donovan *Royal Commission on Trade Unions and Employers' Associations 1965-1968* Cmnd 3623 June 1968

Peter Jenkins *The Battle for Downing Street* Charles Knight 1970

In Place of Strife Cmnd 3888 1968

Joe Rogaly *Grunwick* Penguin 1977

Trade Union Immunities Cmnd 8128 January 1981

Removing Barriers to Employment Cmnd 655 March 1989

Employment in the Ports: The Dock Labour Scheme Cmnd 664 April 1989

Andrew Glyn and Bob Sutcliffe *British Capitalism Workers and the Profits Squeeze* Penguin 1972

Anthony Crosland *The Future of Socialism* 1956

Anthony Crosland *The Conservative Enemy* Jonathan Cape 1962

Martin Jacques and Stuart Hall *Politics of Thatcherism* Lawrence and Wishart in Association with Marxism Today 1983

The Nationalised Industries Cmnd 7131 March 1978

Edmund Dell *The Chancellors* Harper Collins 1996

Public Expenditure to 1979-80 Cmnd 6393 February 1976

Robert Bacon and Walter Eltis *Britain's Economic Problem: Too Few Producers* Macmillan 1976

Emmett Tyrell *The Future That Doesn't Work: Social Democracy's Failures in Britain* Doubleday 1977

Bernard Nossiter *Britain A Future that Works* André Deutsch 1978

The Challenge of North Sea Oil Cmnd. 7143 March 1978

Stephen Powell and Geoff Horton *The Economic Effects of Lower Oil Prices* Treasury Working Paper No 34 HM Treasury April 1985

Nigel Lawson *The View From No 11 Memoirs Of A Tory Radical* Bantam Press 1992

Jock Brue-Gardyne *Mrs Thatcher's First Administration The Prophets Confounded* Macmillan 1984

Leo Pliatzky *Getting and Spending Public Expenditure, Employment and Inflation* Blackwell 1982

The Management of Public Spending HM Treasury 1988

The City A Socialist Approach Labour Party 1981

Kenneth Baker *The Turbulent Years My Life in Politics* Faber and Faber 1993

Duncan Campbell-Smith *Follow the Money Audit Commission, public money and the management of public services* 1983-2008 Allen Lane 2008

Nicholas Ridley *'My Style of Government' The Thatcher Years* Hutchinson 1991

Norman Fowler *Ministers Decide A Memoir Of The Thatcher Years* Chapmans 1991

Paying for Local Government Cmnd9714 1986

Sir Roy Griffiths *Community Care: Agenda For Action* HMSO 1988

David Edgerton *Privatiser and Nationaliser* in *Research Fortnight* April 2013 doi:10.

Jon Agar *Thatcher, Scientist* Notes & Records of the Royal Society

Margaret Thatcher *The Downing Street Years 1979-1990* Harper Collins 1993

New Hope for Britain in Labour Party 1983.

Andrew Adonis and Tim Hames *A Conservative Revolution? The Thatcher-Regan Decade In Perspective* Manchester 1994

Conor Cruise O'Brien *The Decline and Fall of the French Revolution* New York Review of Books 15 February 1990

Francois Furet and Mona Ozouf *A Critical Dictionary of the French Revolution Encyclopaedia of the French Revolution* Harvard 1989

Walter Eltis Financial *Foundations of Industrial Success* The Esmee Fairbairn Lecture Lancaster University 1992

Edmund Dell *A Strange Eventful History Democratic Socialism in Britain* Harper Collins 1999

Lord Bullock *Report of the Committee of Inquiry on Industrial* Cmnd 6706 1977

Industrial Democracy Cmnd 7231 May 1978

The Challenge of North Sea Oil Cmnd 7413 March 1978

John Hills *Thatcherism, New Labour and the Welfare State* CASE Paper LSE August 1998

Working for Patients The Health Service Caring For The 1990s Cmnd 555 January 1989

John Van Reenen *Mrs Thatcher's economic legacy* Vox 11 April 2013

Bibliography

Nicholas Crafts *The Economic Legacy of Mrs Thatcher* 6 Vox April 2013

Margaret Thatcher *Britain and Europe* Bruges Speech Conservative Political Centre 20 September 1988

Anthony Teasdale and Timothy Bainbridge *The Penguin Companion to European Union* Fourth Edition Penguin Books 2012

Index

A

AES. *See* Alternative Economic Strategy
Alternative Economic Strategy 20, 24, 47, 120, 153, 160, 180
Annan, Noel 14
Attlee, Clement 69, 92, 132
Audit Commission 111–112

B

Baker, Kenneth 36, 55, 108
Bank of England 34–35, 37, 80, 90, 132, 142–143
Barber, Anthony 152, 182
Benn, Tony 20, 24, 121, 160
Bevin, Ernest 13, 42
Big Bang 25, 89, 91–92, 95
Blair, Tony 106, 112, 124, 132
Bleaney, Michael 152
Brezhnev, Leonid 121
British Rail 132
Brittan, Leon 165, 168
Britton, Samuel 28
Brockway, Fenner 117
Brown, Gordon 112, 132
Bullock, Lord 152
Bullock Report 82, 152
Bundesbank 33, 35, 38, 160
Bush, George 164
Butskellism 28, 72, 132

C

Callaghan, James 16–17, 44, 46, 49, 53, 73, 77, 81, 99, 120–121, 151, 161, 162
CAP. *See* Common Agricultural Policy
Castle, Barbara 44, 57
Central Electricity Generating Board 51
Centre for Policy Studies 76
Children Act 1989 105, 113
Churchill, Winston 132, 135
City of London 12, 28, 37, 68, 89
Clarke, Kenneth 55
Clegg Commission 49
Clegg, Professor Hugh 49
Cold War 5–6, 136, 167
Common Agricultural Policy 164
Community Charge 109–111, 115
Congdon, Tim 28, 37
Conservative Party 5–6, 15–16, 21, 28–29, 45, 53, 103, 121, 132–133, 135–140, 161–162, 176, 179–181

Crafts, Professor Nicholas 147

Crosland, Anthony 47, 61, 139

D

Davenport, Nicholas 42–43
Delors, Jacques 159–160
d'Estaing, Giscard 157, 162
Diplock, Lord 41, 46
Disraeli, Benjamin 103

Dock Labour Scheme 55, 148, 152
Donovan, Lord Terence 44
Donovan Royal Commission & Report 44, 49
Douglas-Home, Alec 15
Dutch Disease 80–81

E

Economist, The 63, 72, 97
Edelman, Maurice 117
Edgerton, David 125–126
Education Act 1988 113
Eltis, Walter 62, 153
EMS. *See* European Monetary System
ERM. *See* European Exchange Rate Mechanism

European Commission 160, 167, 173, 176
European Exchange Rate Mechanism 22, 33, 115–116, 132, 142, 159–160, 165, 173, 175
European Monetary System 35, 158, 162
European Parliament 173–175
European Social Charter 35–36, 167

F

Falklands War 4, 5–6, 53, 137–138, 167
Financial Times, The 28, 63, 177
Fontainebleau Agreement 164–165
Foot, Michael 46, 120, 154, 157

Fowler, Norman 36, 55, 100, 131, 168
franc fort policy 38, 159
Freidman, Milton 28, 31, 74, 139

G

Gladstone, William 120, 137, 138–139

GLC. *See* Greater London Council
Gorbachev, Mikhail 6

Government Economic Service 8, 34
Greater London Council 25, 112
Green Paper on Monetary Control 31–32
Grunwick dispute 46

H

Hailsham, Lord 136
Hayek, Frederic 72, 135, 139
Heath, Edward 4, 15–17, 20, 24, 29, 31, 45, 52, 54, 72, 161, 177, 182–183
Heffer, Eric 117
Henderson, Sir Nicholas 11–14, 75, 162
Heseltine, Michael 4, 101, 112, 117, 121, 175
Holland, Dr Stuart 160
Housing Act 1980 101
Housing Act 1988 102
Howe, Geoffrey 24, 36, 37, 55, 68, 76, 117, 132, 135, 175, 181
Howell, David 50–51
Hurd, Douglas 36

I

ILEA. *See* Inner London Education Authority
IMF. *See* International Monetary Fund
Industrial Relations Act 1971 24, 45
Inflation 6, 23, 26, 27, 34–41, 42, 44, 47, 48, 61, 69, 71–74, 76, 77, 92, 115, 132, 135, 141–144, 157–159
Inner London Education Authority 25, 112
International Monetary Fund 74, 77, 85

J

Jay, Peter 28, 74, 75
Joseph, Keith 24, 76, 139, 181

K

Keynesianism & neo-Keynesianism 3, 28, 29, 47, 71, 81, 85, 93, 132, 135–136, 139–140, 148, 153–154, 157, 180, 182
Keynes, John Maynard 42
Kinnock, Neil 15, 37, 120–121, 174
Koestler, Arthur 43
Kohl, Helmut 163–164

L

Labour Party 15, 17, 24, 47, 61, 70, 94, 98, 120, 121, 136, 152, 160, 180
Laming, Lord 113
Lamont, Norman 15, 131
Lawson, Nigel 24, 32, 33, 50–54, 69, 101–102, 115, 131, 135, 143–144, 154, 165, 175, 177, 181
Layfield Commission 107
Lever, Harold 32, 117
Liberal Democrats 37, 112
Liberal Party 152
Lilley, Peter 132
Lomax, Rachel 32
London Stock Exchange 25, 89–96

M

Macmillan, Harold 27–28, 43, 104, 132, 180
Major, John 36–37, 131, 161
Marxism 24, 60, 62, 138, 140, 153, 169
Marxism Today 49, 62, 138, 152–153
May, Lord 124
Medium Term Financial Strategy 7, 30, 32, 77, 85, 86
Miners' strike 45, 50, 131, 137
Mitterrand, François 38, 157, 163–164, 167–171, 180
Monetarism 27, 139, 142
Monetary policy 26, 29, 32, 33, 36–37, 39, 49, 71, 142–145, 157, 176–177
Monetary Policy Committee 143
Morrison, Herbert 103
MTFS. *See* Medium Term Financial Strategy

N

National Assistance Act 1948 109
National Coal Board 50–51, 111, 131
National Enterprise Board 47, 81
National Health and Community Care Act 1990 113
National Health Service 97–99, 105, 130, 180
National Health Service and Community Care Act 105
National Union of Mineworkers 45, 50–51, 52–53
New Cambridge 153
New Labour 111, 132
New Statesman 9, 177
NHS. *See* National Health Service
North Sea oil 29, 79, 88, 180
Nossiter, Bernard 75
NUM. *See* National Union of Mineworkers

O

O'Brien, Conor Cruise *169–171*
Office for Budget Responsibility *180*

Oppenheim, Sally *17*
Owen, David *11*

P

"Poll Tax". *See* Community Charge
Prior, James *51*
Private Finance Initiative *131*
Programme Common *157*
PSBR. *See* Public Sector Borrowing Requirement

PSDR. *See* Public Sector Debt Repayment
Public Sector Borrowing Requirement *24, 30, 53, 77, 85*
Public Sector Debt Repayment *85*
Purse, Hugh *168*

R

Reagan, Ronald *6, 138*
Radcliffe Committee *26, 144*
Ridley, Nicholas *24, 36, 55, 181*

Right to Buy scheme *68, 101–103*
Rome Council *175*
Rowthorn, Robert *140, 152*

S

Salisbury, Lord *103, 136*
Scargill, Arthur *51–54, 56, 120*
Schumpeter, Joseph *62, 140, 182*
Science *123–127*
SDP. *See* Social Democrat Party
Social Democrat Party *152*

Social Democrats *48*
Socialism *6, 43, 47, 107, 139*
Strikes *13, 42–44, 46, 48, 55, 56–57, 70, 75, 113, 131, 137. See also* Miners' strike
Sunday Times, The *16, 74*

T

Tebbit, Norman *48, 55, 181*
Thatcherism *115, 131, 135*
Thorneycroft, Peter *28*
Times, The *28, 74, 77*

Trade Disputes Act 1906 *42*
Transport and General Workers Union *42, 52*
TUC *12, 44, 45, 160, 168, 180*

U

UK labour market 8

V

Van Reenan, Professor John
  145–148

Varley, Eric 151
Volcker, Paul 142

W

Washington Post, The 75
Westland crisis 4, 121
White Papers
  In Place of Strife 44, 45, 57
  Nationalised Industries 63
  Public Expenditure to 1979–80 73

  Reform of Social Security 100
  The Challenge of North Sea Oil 81
  Working for Patients 98
Wilson, Harold 16, 44, 46, 57, 73, 120, 121
"Winter of Discontent" 19, 46, 54, 57, 83

Y

Young, Baroness Janet 117
Young, Hugo 169, 177

Young, Lord 55

www.ingramcontent.com/pod-product-compliance
Lightning Source LLC
LaVergne TN
LVHW041542070426
835507LV00011B/879